PAPERIE FOR INSPIRED LIVING

Stationery and Decorations for Weddings,
Parties, and Other Special Occasions

Karen Bartolomei

Photography by Melina Vanderpile

POTTER
CRAFT

NEW YORK

For Bob, my husband, my most trusted advisor, my soul mate, and the love of my life. Your constant strength and support, tireless energy and enthusiasm, endless patience, sense of humor, and unconditional love have enabled me to pursue my passions, launch the business of my dreams, write this book, and maintain my sanity. Because of you I live happier and laugh more than I ever thought possible!

Copyright © 2009 by Karen Bartolomei
Photography copyright © 2009 by Melina Vanderpile

All rights reserved.

Published in the United States by Potter Craft, an imprint of the Crown Publishing Group, a division of Random House, Inc., New York.
www.crownpublishing.com
www.pottercraft.com

POTTER CRAFT and colophon is a registered trademark of Random House, Inc.

Library of Congress Cataloging-in-Publication Data

Bartolomei, Karen.
  Paperie for inspired living : stationery and decorations for every occasion / by Karen Bartolomei. – 1st ed.
      p.   cm.
  ISBN 978-0-307-44943-6
  1. Paper work.   2. Stationery.
  3. Party decorations.   I. Title.
  TT870.B2423   2009
  745.594'1–dc22   2008046083

Printed in China

Design by La Tricia Watford

Contributors
Zibby Right
Kevin Kosbab

Stylists
Karen Bartolomei
Melina Vanderpile

10 9 8 7 6 5 4 3 2 1

First Edition

CONTENTS

INTRODUCTION 4

Your Design Studio 6
The Creative Design Process 8
The Art of Being a Gracious Host 11

EVERYDAY LIVING 14
Personal Stationery 16

CASUAL ENTERTAINING 26
Dinner Party 28
Outdoor Fete 42
Wine Tasting 54
The Oscars 68

SPECIAL OCCASIONS 78
Birthday 80
Anniversary 94
Wedding 104

HOLIDAYS 120
Holiday Gathering 122
New Year's Eve 136

INVITATION GUIDELINES 150
RESOURCES 153
TEMPLATES 156
INDEX 160

Introduction

When was the last time something surprised you, captured your attention, took your breath away, or made you long for more?

In today's busy world, with countless events, e-mails, and errands to contend with, it's a challenge to truly connect with and delight friends and loved ones. Entertaining is a wonderful way to do so. As a gracious host, how do you make your carefully planned event not just enjoyable but truly memorable?

Use paper. From a stunning invitation that announces your fete to a heartfelt thank-you note on monogrammed stationery, paper can make a powerful and lasting impact.

When I receive an invitation, I want to be moved, intrigued, eager to attend the event. Because first impressions are so important, the invitation is the single most important item for every party; it is a window into the upcoming celebration. Make your invitation an expression of your personal style. Capture the spirit and soul of the celebration. Don't miss the opportunity to connect; let the invitation ignite daydreams.

The designs that follow—guest sign-in books, menus, favor tags, programs, thank-you notes—should reflect the design established by your invitation and tell the story of your celebration through words and imagery. All of these pieces, which together comprise the paperie suite, should send a cohesive message and blend seamlessly with your event design. If done with style and verve, your creations will become treasured keepsakes. Your guests will compliment you endlessly on your thoughtfulness, impeccable taste, and amazing talent.

I founded Grapevine, my couture paperie design studio, on the belief that the paperie experience should not end after the invitations are received. Too often, the design of the paperie suite is not given the attention it deserves. More than just paper and ink, it is a tangible representation that will last long after memories of the gathering fade. I pour my heart and soul into my designs. My wish is for each individual to be captivated by the invitation, to feel the excitement and energy of the celebration from the moment the invitation arrives, and to eagerly anticipate what is to come. The indulgence continues when guests discover pieces of the suite in unexpected places throughout the evening. And finally, when they receive their thank-you note, they will know their host has thought of every detail. Every client I've had the pleasure of working with over the years has been astonished at the emotional response their paperie has evoked, from their grandparents and co-workers to even the most "no-frills" men on the guest list.

Whether you're planning a wedding, hosting a holiday party, or throwing a birthday bash, push the envelope with your designs. Delight your guests, from the first glimpse of the invitation envelope and the carefully chosen postage stamps to the splash of color the menus provide at each place setting. The magic and the memories of every event are in the details. Your paperie should express your individuality. Take chances. Draw inspiration from the unexpected—graffiti on the side of a building, celebrity fashion on the red carpet, texture from a rural landscape, interesting shapes from modern architecture, a thrift-store coat pattern—and translate it into functional yet provocative design. Choose materials and design elements with confidence, and combine them so they'll make beautiful sense together. Flawlessly. Fearlessly. Glamorously.

Don't feel compelled to follow every project to the letter. The instructions in this book are meant to teach you basic design principles and techniques, to spark your imagination and turn your artistic vision into vivid reality. Use them as a guide and a creative springboard, and then let your imagination go.

Be passionate about your paperie. Extraordinary design and attention to detail will make every celebration an event to remember!

Your Design Studio

Even if it's just a corner of your kitchen, your design space can be the perfect place to dream and let your imagination flow, especially with proper organization and all the right tools.

Surround yourself with good design: Pin up fresh fabric swatches, tear sheets from magazines, photographs of far-away places, fun fonts from birthday cards or clothing tags, foreign postage, paint swatches, and old buttons or postcards found at a local thrift shop. Stock nearby shelves with books and magazines on art and design, royalty-free images and il-lustrations, typeface catalogs, and ephemera.

Materials and Tools

I use some tools and adhesives once a month and others every day. Keeping this in mind when purchasing and storing my tools is key to successful organization. The general rule I employ is whatever I use every day—scissors, bone folders, craft knives and blades, double-sided tape—I keep within arm's reach of my work surface. The rest of the items can be stored on shelves or in labeled boxes, clear containers, or open bins.

Making Memories and Martha Stewart Crafts™—both available for purchase online—have some of the best tools and adhesives on the market today.

BASIC MATERIALS

- Text-weight paper (perfect for letterhead, scrolls, mailing labels, program pages, wrapping paper, flyers, and copies) and cover-weight paper (or card stock; used for invitations, booklet covers, business and note cards, pocket folders, menus, and brochures). 8.5" x 11" (21.5cm x 28cm) sheets of 80-pound (36.3kg) weight in both text and cover (card stock) are recommended for these projects because they are the most common and versatile weights in the U.S. Most stationery and craft stores (including Paper-Source.com, thepapermillstore.com, Paper-Papers.com) sell their whites

and colors in 80-pound text and cover. There are heavier and lighter versions of each, but the lighter weights are too flimsy and lack the quality necessary for anything but photocopies. Heavier text weights are harder to find, and heavier cover weights tend to jam home printers. In the U.S., paper weight is based on a carton of 500 large *uncut* sheets of paper. If you are wondering how cover weight can be heavier than text weight when both cartons weigh 80 pounds, it's because letter-sized sheets of cover weight are cut down from a 20" x 26" (51cm x 66cm) sheet, and letter-sized sheets of text weight are cut down from a larger 25" x 38" (63.5cm x 96.5cm) sheet.

- Envelopes (most versatile sizes to keep on hand: 4 Baro-nial, A2, A6, A7, A9, #10 open-end business, 5¾" and 6½" [14.5cm and 16.5cm] square envelopes. [See envelope size chart on page 152.])
- Large decorative sheets of handmade and printed paper
- Ribbon, cord, thread, yarn, beading wire, and raffia
- Findings such as beads, flat-back crystals, brass upholstery tacks, buttons, buckles, and clasps
- Royalty-free artwork books and CDs, typeface, catalogs, magazines, and ephemera
- Fabric: silk, felt, linen, netting, denim, lace, and faux fur

> Music is one of the most important things to have in your creative space. Setting your cre-ativity to music can lift your spirits, drown out distractions, and get your creative juices flowing.

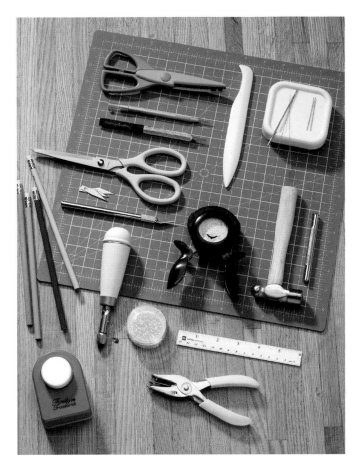

BASIC TOOLS

- Self-healing cutting mat (most versatile, transportable size: 18" x 24" [45.5cm x 61 cm])
- Craft scissors (for use with paper and card stock)
- Fabric and ribbon scissors (ultra sharp, for fabric and ribbon only)
- Decorative-edge scissors, such as pinking shears
- Craft knife and replacement blades
- Steel ruler with cork backing (most versatile length: 18" [45.5cm])
- Hole punches: ⅛", ¼", and ½" (3mm, 6mm, 13mm) single-hole hand punches, large circle and decorative hole punches, corner-rounding punch
- Making Memories Instant Setter with three-hole punching tips (spring loaded for easy hole punching and eyelet setting anywhere on your document)
- Eyelet setter, hammer, and self-healing mat
- Bookbinder's awl
- Beading needles, large-eye ribbon/yarn needles, standard sewing needles
- Bone folder
- #2 pencils
- ArtGum and Design® kneaded rubber erasers
- Paintbrushes (bristle and foam)

BASIC ADHESIVES

- Aleene's® Tacky Glue (white, water soluble, all-purpose craft glue)
- Super 77™ spray mount (for precise permanent positioning of artwork and laminating multiple sheets of paper together)
- Acid-free photo mount spray
- Double-sided tape
- Glue stick
- Hot-glue gun (for application of glue and wax seals)
- Zots™ (small, large, and three-dimensional dots)
- Adhesive remover for easy cleanup

Finally, a note on work surfaces: Crafting is messy. Hot glue, spray mount, double-sided tape, paint, and ribbon snippings get everywhere when I am creating, so the surfaces on which I design and assemble are built for craft. I have two six-foot stainless-steel work tables set up at counter height with four stools so I can stand or sit, depending upon the assembly. And cleaning up after every project is a must! I have three trash bins in my studio, one each for bottles and cans, paper scraps, and nonrecyclable items.

The Creative Design Process

It helps to come up with a creative vision for your celebration before designing your paperie suite. Your vision will affect your choice of color, fonts, imagery, paper, and assembly. Close your eyes and picture your event. Think of who, what, where, and why you are celebrating. What is the mood, the formality, the size of the party? Is this an intimate, low-key celebration in a candlelit garden, or is it everyone you know at an energized, South Beach–infused soiree in a club setting? How do you want guests to feel when they enter the party and when they leave?

Begin by picking a color palette. Color sets the tone and formality of your event and can even change the mood of the celebration.

Next, choose a theme, logo, and motif. As a graphic designer, I base my decisions for theme and logo on the location; the formality and mood of the event; personalities of the honorees as well as the occasion being celebrated; budget; the color, décor, and architecture of the surroundings; the time of year; the age and interests of guests attending; and my clients' personal passions, hobbies, and tastes.

START WITH YOUR INVITATION

Using your chosen elements, start composing your designs beginning with the invitation.

Pick a shape. Although your invitation must meet postal mailing requirements, that does not mean it has to be sent in an envelope or be rectangular in shape. To be sure your invitation is mailable before recreating it for your entire guest list, take one to the post office for approval or read through the USPS mailing requirements brochure.

Choose typefaces. Typography is the most important visual element in design. You are not only imparting information about location, time, and date, but you are also relaying the formality, character, and mood of the celebration while welcoming, intriguing, and exciting guests. Choose fonts that are reflective of your theme and easy to read.

Incorporate imagery. After laying out your type, it's time to add imagery. The glue that holds your design together, imagery adds visual chemistry, anchors text blocks, creates visual flow, and draws the eye to the most important information.

I have spent many years seeking out copyright-free original artwork—new and old—to use in my designs. There are plenty of resources available, but many charge hefty fees for use, which may be acceptable for corporate work but are prohibitively expensive for your twentieth birthday or Oscar celebration invitations. The designs in this book use the best image sources that I have found (logos, photography, clipart and vintage illustrations). The websites listed in the Artwork Sources (page 155) have low or no download fees, feature simple and effective search functions, and contain a large collection of useful artwork that you can use without worry of copyright infringement.

There are many other innovative, inexpensive ways to incorporate artwork in your designs. Create the art or photographs yourself. Scour flea markets, eBay.com and antique stores for centuries-old books with interesting title pages, letters and illustrations. Hire a professional illustrator, calligrapher, or cartographer to create an original work of art or font for your designs. Scan artwork and place it in your document in the color of your choice, collage the art as is, or create a custom rubber stamp of the art and brand it on all of your pieces. See page 153 for a full list of my favorite resources and page 155 for sources of the artwork used in each project.

Note: The art you choose to include in your projects may be protected by copyright. Copyright laws are complicated and confusing, so it is always best to use your own original art (photographs, illustrations, logos) or art that is in the public domain. If you do use copyrighted art, please make sure your use does not violate any copyright laws; a summary is available on websites such as www.copyright.gov.

Pick your paper. When working on a do-it-yourself project, I find that using a base of white or cream paper is the best option, allowing the most versatility and readability in design. Adding color in envelopes, liners, layers, and embellishments brings life and excitement to your design with little additional cost.

Your paper choice communicates much more than the logistical details, so choose wisely. Textured paper or soft cotton paper with natural fibers or floral inclusions reflects the tone of an outdoor or casual celebration, while smooth paper or coated paper with a slight shimmer has a sleeker look and sets the stage for a formal gathering or evening event.

FORM VERSUS FUNCTION

Sometimes what is in my mind or on my computer screen does not translate well in the real world. When it comes time for assembly, be prepared to make a few alterations to the design. The font you chose may look clumsy next to a delicate flower petal, but if you make the font smaller it may be hard to read. Woven ribbon binding may look stunning through five holes at the top of your program, but the time it takes to punch the holes and thread the ribbon on fifty programs can be excessive. Be open to change and be flexible.

Don't stop with your first design concept. Show it to others to solicit their feedback. The best designs are not always the early ones. If you fine-tune your choices, rework your ideas, and keep an open mind throughout the entire creative process, you will inevitably come up with the perfect design for every occasion.

THE BIGGER PICTURE

When creating your paperie, don't stop at the invitation; that would be like ending dinner after the appetizer. It will leave guests unfulfilled and wanting more.

Once you have established your invitation design, work backward to your save-the-date and then carry the theme forward with your event accessories and thank-you notes, pulling patterns, imagery, font choices, and color combinations from your invitation. Mix and match them throughout your paperie. Add interest by choosing different shapes, folds, assembly, and bindings.

When you have completed your paperie suite, put all the pieces together. Take a bird's-eye view of the entire suite. If the big picture feels disjointed, you can rework the designs that don't fit well so your celebration story flows seamlessly from piece to piece.

choosing the perfect color scheme

Here are some tried and true suggestions for color:

Winter

All white (ethereal and heavenly)

Black and white (timeless)

Silver or flannel gray and white

Plum, silver, and mauve (contemporary glamour)

Cobalt or ice blue and white (a great alternative to red and green, especially for Hanukkah celebrations)

Spring

Easter colors: pastel hues of purple, green, blue, pink, and yellow

Robin's egg blue or lilac paired with brown (simple and classic)

Celadon and lavender

Hot pink and white (playful)

Blush pink and butter yellow (warmth and romance)

Sorbet colors

Summer

Red, white, and blue (patriotic)

Royal blue and white (nautical)

Citrus colors: orange, yellow, and lime

Cranberry red and sky blue

Orange and raspberry

Caribbean blue and orange

Fall

Chocolate brown and tan or beige (rustic)

Fall foliage: deep red, orange, gold, and brown

Jewel tones: emerald green and navy or cranberry and plum

Celadon and burgundy or brown

Sage green and taupe (harmonious)

Anytime

Orange and gray

Blush pink and gold (softness and royalty)

Red and white

Ecru with black, navy, or brown

Royal purple and cream

Slate blue and silver (conservative and sophisticated)

Monochromatic color schemes (pairing a single hue with white makes any color modern, sophisticated, and chic)

NOTE: As with all light colors, large solid blocks of color work beautifully, but the thin lines in type create an optical illusion that makes light-colored fonts very difficult to read. To keep text legible, it is important to make the color of type a shade or two darker than artwork.

proper postage

Don't settle for postage designs that don't complement your invitations. Try to find stamps with color- and theme-appropriate artwork, matching both your outer and RSVP envelope postage. If you are unable to find a match in the current stamp releases, purchase vintage stamps at championstamp.com or create your own design on zazzle.com.

Boxed invitations and envelopes that are more than ¼" (6mm) thick must be hand sorted. Thick card stock or multiple cards can quickly push the weight of your invitation over 1 oz. (28g). Square envelopes cannot be scanned and bar-coded by the postal machines. All of these design sizes require additional postage. Postcards require a lower first class rate for mailing. To determine the proper postage for mailing your invitation, take one fully assembled invitation to the post office and have it weighed with all enclosures and appropriate postage.

When mailing your invitations, have the post office hand-cancel the invitations with a rubber stamp. This will ensure that the automated canceling machines will not print an unattractive bar code across the bottom of the envelope, and it will prevent damage to the invitation.

lining envelopes

Spice up any invitation or thank-you note by adding an envelope liner. Use custom-printed light card stock for a luxurious feel or try textured, handmade, patterned, or tissue paper. Pick a color that matches your invitation text, a pattern that matches your party's formality or theme, a textured paper, or your monogram, repeated. Envelope liners easily add weight and extravagance to any announcement.

To create a lining for an envelope, follow these simple steps:

1 Choose an envelope liner paper.

2 Use a spare blank envelope as your template and lay it with the flap open on your chosen liner paper.

3 With a pencil, lightly trace the shape of the envelope on the back of your liner paper.

4 Use craft scissors or a craft knife, a ruler, and a cutting mat to cut the shape out. You will need to trim the shape about ½" (13mm) from the edges of the point of the flap, ¼" (6mm) from the left and right sides, and ⅛" (3mm) from the bottom of the envelope.

5 Line both edges of the pointed envelope flap with double-sided tape, slide the liner into the envelope, and center it. Then press the liner down to adhere it to the envelope.

If you decide to line with tissue paper, use a glue stick instead of double-sided tape. For sheer or thin paper, use Incredi Tape™: It's ultra thin, practically invisible behind sheer vellum, and acid-free. For large jobs, consider using a Scotch ATG double-sided tape gun available at bindingsource.com. Simply press the trigger and run the tip of the gun along your paper to adhere the tape and pull off the backing in one quick motion with no mess or clean up.

The Art of Being a Gracious Host

Creating the complete experience for your guests is key for a memorable gathering. If you want your party to have the "remember when" effect—meaning friends and family will be talking about it fondly for years to come—the most important thing to keep in mind throughout your planning and execution is to make your guests feel comfortable.

When my husband and I threw our first party as a couple, we knew our friends from all different segments of our lives and our two families might feel awkward mixing and mingling, so to break the ice after a long sit-down dinner (which slowed the momentum of the evening), we hired a professional comedian who willingly worked with us to create twenty minutes of personalized stand-up about our relationship, our friends, family, and our city in general. At the end of the twenty minutes, everyone was whistling, laughing, and clapping—a perfect segue into an evening of dancing. As people continued their applause, we turned up the music and played three dance songs back to back. Our guests, who normally don't dance, charged the dance floor and stayed there for the next four hours. And we saw conversations spark between people who we thought would never speak to each other.

Your event is not simply a gathering to honor someone or something; it is history, tradition, personalities, and relationships—it is shared moments between friends and family. Music and refreshments aren't the only details to consider when throwing a party. The evening's journey can encompass everything from paperie to cocktails, from the coat check to the restroom amenities. Make it a feast for the senses: beautiful décor, the right entertainment, great conversation, delicious food, fabulous cocktails, moving music, and so much more. Your guests will feel they are not merely a part of the celebration, but the most important part.

Many of us are working on tight budgets either with time, money, or both. So consider the following details when planning your next gathering. You don't have to include everything; concentrating on fewer details and doing them well is much better than overextending yourself or incorporating everything half-heartedly.

Choose a theme. Whether it's a holiday, time of year, location, historic event, color or pattern, flower, monogram, or logo, repeat your theme throughout the event in subtle ways to unify your celebration.

Define your style. Be it organic, chic, lush, exotic, or minimalist, defining the style and formality of the gathering will help you produce the perfect party, from flowers and linens to music and lighting.

Use your paperie. Tell the complete celebration story to your guests through your paperie suite. It will invite them, lead them through the evening, and send them on their way with beautiful keepsakes that will tell of memories that last a lifetime!

Decorate. Use warm and inviting décor that coordinates with existing architecture and interior design. Dramatic centerpieces and small arrangements scattered in unexpected places, colorful linens, and coordinating place settings and serving pieces create strong visual stimuli. Don't forget to adorn your serving trays, bathroom counter, and bar!

Save money and choose non-floral décor. Use shells and stones, grapevine, bittersweet or pussy-willow branches, fresh fruit and vegetables, feathers, leaves, acorns, bundles of wheat, crystals, crepe-paper flowers, candles, potted plants, and vibrant fabrics. Most of these can be used year after year.

While much of my own décor comes from estate sales, flea markets, and antique shops, I do find trendy and conventional staple items at Pier 1 Imports, Home Goods, Target, and IKEA. Bargain shopping, buying in bulk, and accenting your purchases with unique finds and pieces from your own collection can be important when keeping the budget in check. It allows you to create a totally custom, personalized look without a huge expense.

Set the mood with lighting. The right lighting will transform a room. Turn off the overhead and direct lighting. Scatter lanterns, hurricane vases filled with candles, and luminarias around outdoor seating areas. Try winding long strings of twinkling lights through the trees or even indoors. Replace harsh lighting with 25-watt soft white bulbs, or soft pink or amber 25-watt bulbs (from LightBulbsDirect.com), and don't forget the unscented votives. They cast a romantic glow over everything.

Consider the seating. Create gathering and sitting areas throughout your home, for the bar, food service, entertainment, and music. Offer quiet nooks for people to have intimate conversations. Comfortable seating will make guests stay longer.

de-mystify the dress code

While it is not necessary to tell your guests how to dress for your event, they will most likely appreciate the subtle cue. Specifying attire on your invitation is a considerate gesture that may spare your guests unnecessary embarrassment and save you time by reducing the number of phone calls you receive from invitees to clarify what is expected.

White tie
Translation: The most formal dress reserved for evening weddings. Men: Tuxedos with white tie, vest, shirt. Women: Floor-length gowns. Variations: Full dress.

Black tie
Translation: Formal day and evening affairs. Tuxedos and gowns of various lengths.

Black tie optional
Translation: Elegant and glamorous but not stuffy. Dark suit or tuxedo and gowns of various lengths or formal evening separates. Variations: Black tie invited, Creative black tie, Black tie preferred, Texas tuxedo, Formal Attire.

Festive attire
Translation: Playful cocktail attire, something modern with a bit of sparkle. Variations: Holiday chic, Cocktail attire, Simply fabulous, Gorgeous garb, Dressed to kill.

Suit and tie
Translation: Men: Just as it reads. Women: Pulled-together, semiformal attire. Variations: Jacket requested, Dark and chic, After five, Semiformal.

Casual chic
Translation: Men: Dress Shirt and slacks. Women: Flirty dresses, bare legs, fun accessories. A mix of formal and informal elements. Variations: Informal, Smart casual, Dressy casual, Casual threads, Informally fabulous, Simple and chic, Resortwear, Beach chic, Garden party, No jeans.

Business attire
Translation: Suits in bright colors or paired with fun accessories. Variations: Business casual, Urban chic, City dress, Downtown chic.

Come as you are
Translation: Endless possibilities. Dressy or casual, laid back but not sloppy. Variations: Dress as you please, Smart attire, Garden Chic.

Be ready for your guests. Expect that some of your guests will arrive early and some will most definitely be late. With this in mind, make sure you are dressed and ready at least a half hour before the time printed on your invitations. Early arrivals can help you finish setting up. If you are having a formal sit-down dinner, hold off on serving the first course no longer than fifteen minutes for late guests.

Remember your guests' children. If you choose to invite children to your event, make plans for the comfort of both the children and their parents. Hire a babysitter. Have special rooms: one for games and movies, and the other for sleeping or breastfeeding. Give the children a special table with all the arts-and-crafts fixings (making sure that all supplies are non-permanent/washable). Serve them kids' food like hot dogs, PB&J, chicken fingers—things that aren't too messy but are fun to eat. (Be sure to ask parents about their favorites and their dietary restrictions beforehand.)

The majority of parents relish the idea of a few hours away from the kids for adult conversation and entertainment, so it is perfectly acceptable to not invite children. Spread the word personally well in advance so your friends with kids can plan for child care, and be prepared for last-minute cancelations if their babysitter backs out.

Welcome your guests. Adorn the entrance: It is the perfect welcome and makes guests feel at home instantly. Try a swag over the archway, a wreath on the door, live musicians, or luminarias flanking the walkway. To reduce hassle and chaos, try to situate the coat check or closet near the door. Offer a shoe check with flip-flops for outdoor gatherings. Then pamper your guests throughout the evening with small, unexpected details: custom-printed cocktail napkins, amenities baskets in the restrooms, milk and cookies at the end of the night.

Serve cocktails. Though the concept is not a new one, the signature cocktail is a must at every event. You will find fun ways to add signature drinks to your celebration throughout this book. Theme-inspired cocktails break the ice, infuse your party with more of your personality and celebration theme, and can even add a splash of color!

Greet your guests when they arrive with a tray of signature cocktails or wine. Set up a full bar in an empty corner and provide all of the accoutrements, from mixers to garnishes. Plan for the average guest to consume approximately one cocktail or glass of wine per hour. If you have a large beer-drinking crowd, plan on an average of two bottles of beer per guest per hour. Create pitchers or decorative jugs and punch bowls for your signature drinks to reduce the wait time. If at all possible, hire a bartender! They can be hired for as little as $100 for four hours and really keep the alcohol flowing and the bar line moving. Don't allow a tip jar to be placed on the bar. Settle the gratuity with the bartender at the end of the evening so your guests will not feel pressure to pull out their wallets when they order their drinks.

Serve interesting non-alcoholic drinks for drivers, non-drinkers, expectant mothers, and under-aged guests. Serve raspberry-infused lemonade in the spring, peach-flavored iced tea in the summer, spiced apple cider in the fall, and mint-infused hot cocoa or cappuccino in the winter. And don't forget glass pitchers of spring water garnished with slices of fresh cucumber, orange, apple, and lime.

Entertain. Break the ice and keep guests entertained with surprises and amusements throughout the evening. Consider hiring entertainers like a live band, an emcee to host a roast, a professional chef to make crepes and omelets at the end of the night, a professional dealer for a casino night, an accordion player or wandering musician, a pianist, disc jockey, cigar roller, belly dancer, stand-up comedian, fortune teller or palm reader, tattoo or henna artist, silhouette or caricature artist, a sommelier or a performing bartender. Or pull out all the stops and hire a fireworks specialist. Rent a Karaoke machine, flavored oxygen bar, or old-time photo booth, or a horse and carriage for hay or sleigh rides. Pamper your sports fanatics by designating a room with the game on TV so they can check the score throughout the night. The point is to create anticipation and keep the momentum of the party going with an evening full of surprises and highlights.

Play music. Music should play continuously throughout the event. So when the band takes a break, have your own music ready to fill in. If you choose to play your own music, rather than hiring live musicians, create mix CDs or playlists on your iPod or MP3 player beforehand for different segments of the evening. Start off with lively themed music as guests arrive for cocktails (New Orleans Zydeco for your Riesling and Cajun wine pairing dinner or steel drum and reggae for your outdoor gathering). Tone the music tempo and volume down during dinner and then pick it up again after dinner with a mix of music your guests will know and love. As things are winding down, play instrumental or romantic songs to end the evening. It moves guests through the evening seamlessly and lets them know what to expect. Music can create a mood, but it should not be so loud that it drowns out conversation.

Offer food. I cannot stress enough how important food is at your gathering. It keeps guests happy and going strong throughout the evening, especially at a cocktail party. Be sure to ask guests to inform you in advance of any food allergies or dietary restrictions.

Sit-down meals can be drawn out and tiresome; try livening things up by serving local cuisine or food that follows the theme of your celebration. Even finger foods should be well thought-out. They should not be messy, hard to eat, or full of garlic. Plan on six to ten pieces per person. Passed hors d'oeuvres will pamper your guests, but you can also consider a stationary display. It will allow guests to help themselves, providing a place other than the bar to congregate and mingle.

Snacks for the end of the night/early morning are always a smart choice. Have a local Chinese restaurant deliver takeout, make a McDonald's run, serve crepes and hot chocolate, or put out some mini hamburgers and canned soda. Any type of heavy finger food and caffeinated beverage after midnight will slow down the consumption of alcohol and help guests stay awake on the journey home.

Have fun. Take time to enjoy your party. Guests will only have as much fun as you're having. Don't start washing dishes and cleaning up after food is served; this is always a downer and can end a party quickly.

Express your gratitude. Parting gifts and favors say thank you to your guests for attending and enriching your life. These tokens don't have to be expensive, but unexpected gifts, thoughtfully wrapped, are the perfect end to a perfect evening. The best advice I have for gift giving is make it useful or edible. When questioning what to give your guests, you must ask yourself, "Is this something I myself would keep/want/use?"

Cleverly packaged favors on each place setting add a splash of color to your table décor. They can also create visual impact displayed on a shelf or console in a forgotten corner. Put them in a basket at the door or coat room so guests can take one as they leave or, if you have a valet service, ask them to place the favors on the dash of each car when guests come to claim their vehicles.

EVERYDAY LIVING

Personal Stationery

Custom Paperweight 18

Business Card 20

Gift Tag. 21

Letterhead and Overlay. 22

Mailing Label 24

Custom-Printed Envelope 24

Fold-Over Note Card. 25

Flat Note Card. 25

A STATIONERY SUITE—LETTERHEAD, BUSINESS OR CALLING CARDS, ENVELOPES, mailing labels, gift tags, and note cards—does not need a hefty price tag to impress. It should, however, be well thought-out and reflective of you. Your choice of color, font, and imagery will evoke emotions from the recipient, and make a lasting impact.

Not everyone fits the mold catered to by stationery companies. We are made up of many complex characteristics, experiences, memories, and feelings, all constantly evolving. A design that someone else created for the masses can be too generic and predictable. On the other hand, selecting a single emblem or style to personify you can be overwhelming. The paperie designs in this chapter will illustrate how to blend elements and colors across multiple pieces to vary and enhance your look on paper.

I found the inspiration for my personal suite in my workspace. I surround myself with things of beauty to remain continuously stimulated, uplifted, and inspired. My love of antiques, interior design, and ephemera shines through all my workspace components. My desktop is an old wooden door with the handle intact. Aged silver compotes hold my pins and elastics. My mail is sorted in an antique sterling toast rack. I organize wax and seals in a silver-plated breadbasket. Ribbons, writing instruments, and postage, all color coordinated, decorate the shelves and custom glass paperweights keep things in place. I regularly update and rotate these things for minimum clutter and maximum fresh perspective. Likewise, your personal suite designs should come to life in your workspace. Blow up monograms and frame them. Scatter butterflies around as if they are floating in a glorious paper garden. Display tools and materials in beautiful antique containers with butterflies perched on the edges.

Then start soul-searching and brainstorming: Who are you? Make a list of words that describe you. What are your favorite things:

plants, animals, vacation spots, activities, colors, and patterns? Research your family crest, your ancestors, and the meaning behind your name or your favorite color.

Symbols

Pore through books (old and new), art sources, trade magazines, and websites in search of the perfect symbol for your stationery. I couldn't decide between vintage etchings of my first initial and butterflies, so I used both.

Whether formal or casual, monograms convey sophistication, elegance, and thoughtfulness. Choosing your initial or monogram as a motif for your stationery suite is the obvious choice, but it doesn't have to be boring. You can choose a rare font, a vintage ornamental letter, or a two- or three-letter monogram, or you can have a calligrapher or illustrator design a couture monogram just for you. I chose several ornamental Ks, alternating their color and placement.

The butterfly is a symbol of beauty in nature. It is perfection in color, shape, pattern, and symmetry. Representing femininity, youthfulness, metamorphosis, and new life, it is an emblem of change and rebirth. The butterflies in this design gracefully flit and float around monograms and text, adding movement to the designs. Infuse new life into each piece by changing color and composition to create balance.

Color

We are surrounded by color every day, but we tend to look past it and often miss its subtle hues. We ignore how different shades make us feel. But color is powerful. Color is nonverbal communication. It helps to understand what various colors symbolize before you choose your palette.

Colors have special meaning in a logo, family crest, or coat of arms. They mean different things in different cultures, but over the years, nearly every culture has associated gold with the sun, silver with the moon, blue with the sky, and white with purity. Whatever the meaning, you can liven up any design with vivid colors like the navy and kelly green combination featured in this suite.

custom paperweight

Magnify your motif under crystal or glass paperweights to keep paper piles in place and add visual stimuli to your work area in an organized, uncluttered, and functional way. There are so many different paperweight kits to choose from (try Photoweights.com), you will have a hard time buying just one! Simply draw crop marks with the dimensions specified in the directions for your paperweight kit, set the type and graphics, print, and follow the kit's instructions.

Business Card

(Makes 6 Business Cards)

Your business card design conveys a great deal more than just your name and contact information. It is a miniature representation of your style and personality that will be kept for years, so don't miss this opportunity to make a positive and lasting impression.

MATERIALS
- 1 sheet 8½" x 11" (21.5cm x 28cm) white card stock
- 6 navy blue business card envelopes, measuring 2¼" x 3½" (5.5cm x 9cm)

TOOLS
- Craft knife, self-healing cutting mat, and ruler
- White gel pen

ARTWORK
- Monogram clipart

INSTRUCTIONS

1 Create an 8½" x 11" (21.5cm x 28cm) document in your computer page layout or word-processing program and draw crop marks for 6 business cards that each measure 2" (5cm) wide x 3½" (9cm) high.

2 Scan and place your monogram and text inside the crop marks for each card. Be sure to include your name, mailing address, home phone and cell phone numbers, and e-mail address.

3 Print the document on the sheet of white card stock. Trim your cards to the crop marks.

4 Slide each business card into a navy blue business card envelope. For a special touch, personalize each business card envelope with the recipient's name using a white gel pen.

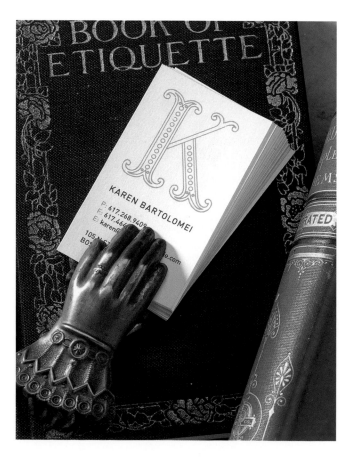

Gift Tag

(Makes 12 Tags)

Put as much thought into the presentation of your gift as the gift itself. Delicate butterflies and vintage letters are dramatically printed in reverse on vibrant green and blue backgrounds. These sweet little cards, tucked into sheer glassine envelopes, are the perfect topping for any present.

MATERIALS
- 1 sheet 8½" x 11" (21.5cm x 28cm) white card stock
- 12 glassine envelopes, 2¾" (6.8mm) square

TOOLS
- Craft knife, self-healing cutting mat, and ruler

ARTWORK
- Butterfly art from a vintage book; monogram clipart

INSTRUCTIONS

1 Create an 8½" x 11" (21.5cm x 28cm) document in your computer page layout or word-processing program.

2 Draw crop marks for 12 gift tags, each measuring 2½" (6.5cm) square. Draw a solid blue box behind 6 tags and solid green box behind 6 tags making sure your solid backgrounds extend approximately ⅛" (3cm) past your crop marks.

3 Scan and place your monogram and butterfly art inside the crop marks for each card. Reverse the color of the artwork to white.

4 Print the document on the sheet of white card stock. Trim your tags to the crop marks.

Letterhead and Overlay

(Makes 1 Letterhead Sheet and 1 Overlay Sheet)

For a refreshing change of pace, skip the e-mail or text message and add warmth to your personal communication with a hand-written letter on personalized letterhead. Add softness and depth to your letterhead with a sheer overlay that complements and enhances your design.

MATERIALS
- 1 sheet 8½" × 14" (21.5cm × 35.5cm) white text-weight paper
- 1 sheet 11" × 17" (28cm × 43cm) 29-lb translucent vellum paper

(inkjet or laser compatible, depending on your printer)

TOOLS
- Craft knife, self-healing cutting mat, and ruler

ARTWORK
- Butterfly art from a vintage book; monogram clipart; hand-drawn outline of leaves and flowers for floral background

INSTRUCTIONS

Letterhead

1 Create an 8½" x 14" (21.5cm x 35.5cm) document in your computer page layout or word-processing program and draw a frame measuring 8½" x 11" (21.5cm x 28cm). (You may want to print a test page to see how close you are able to print to the left and right edges of the page.)

2 Scan the butterflies and floral design and place your artwork and text inside the frame. Allow your floral design to bleed outside the top and bottom of the frame. For the letterhead, be sure to include your name, mailing address, home phone and cell phone numbers, and your e-mail address. (If your desktop printer can accommodate tabloid sized sheets, simply create an 11" x 17" (28cm x 43cm) document, draw crop marks measuring 8½" x 11" (21.5cm x 28cm), and allow your floral artwork to bleed outside the crop marks.)

3 Print the document on a sheet of white text-weight paper. Trim the top and bottom of the letterhead inside the frame.

Overlay

1 Repeat steps 1 and 2: Create another 8½" x 14" (21.5cm x 35.5cm) document and place the artwork inside the frame, allowing it to bleed.

2 Trim the vellum sheet to 8½" x 14" (21.5cm x 35.5cm). Print the document on the sheet of vellum paper. Trim the top and bottom of the overlay inside the frame.

Mailing Label and Custom-Printed Envelope

(Makes 4 Mailing Labels—2 Large and 2 Small—and 1 Envelope

Spice up your mailing envelopes and packages instantly with custom mailing labels. They personalize any packaging, look fabulous on colored envelopes, and ensure that you pen the recipient's address on straight, evenly spaced lines. Or, to make a sophisticated statement, custom-print your logo onto the front or back of an envelope. The #10 envelope is the most common business-sized envelope and is the perfect fit for your letterhead sheet when folded into thirds.

MATERIALS

• 1 sheet 8½" x 11" (21.5cm x 28cm) white crack-and-peel label stock
• 1 white #10 business envelope (4⅛" x 9½" [10.5cm x 24cm])

TOOLS

• Craft knife, self-healing cutting mat, and ruler

ARTWORK

• Vintage butterfly art and monogram clipart

INSTRUCTIONS

Mailing Labels

1 Create an 8½" x 11" (21.5cm x 28cm) document and draw crop marks for 4 mailing labels, 2 measuring 4¼" (11cm) wide x 2½" (6.5cm) high for small packages, and 2 measuring 5¾" (14.5cm) wide x 2½" (6.5cm) high for larger packages.

2 Scan your monogram, butterflies, and floral design, and place your artwork and text inside the crop marks. Include your name and return address, and rules or lines for writing the delivery address by hand.

3 Print the document on the sheet of white crack-and-peel label stock. Trim your tags to the crop marks. Leave the protective backing on the labels until you're ready to use them.

Envelope

1 Create a document for your #10 envelope measuring 9½" (24cm) wide x 4⅛" high (10.5cm). Typeset the return address with the same font from the letterhead.

2 Scan and place monogram artwork above the address in the top left corner.

3 Print the envelope using the manual feed tray on your printer.

Note Card

(Makes 1 Fold-Over Card or 2 Flat Cards)

In an age when the art of the handwritten note has almost become obsolete, there's no better way to say thank you or let someone know you're thinking of them than to send a personalized note card—folded or flat. It is a gift in itself. (Shown at top left of page 19.)

MATERIALS

Fold-Over Card

• 1 sheet 8½" x 14"
(21.5cm x 35.5cm)
white card stock

• 1 sheet 8½" x 11"
(21.5cm x 28cm) decorative
text-weight paper

• 1 navy blue A2 envelope
(4⅜" x 5¾"
[11.1cm x 14.5cm])

Flat Card

• 1 sheet 8½" x 11"
(21.5cm x 28cm)
white card stock

• 2 sheets 8½" x 11"
(21.5cm x 28cm) decorative
text-weight paper

• 2 navy blue A2 envelopes
(4⅜" x 5¾"
[11.1cm x 14.5cm])

TOOLS

• Craft knife, self-healing
cutting mat, and ruler

ARTWORK

• Monogram clipart and hand-
drawn outline of leaves and
flowers for floral background
of fold-over card

• Butterfly art from a vintage
book and monogram clipart
for flat card

INSTRUCTIONS

Fold-Over Card

1 Create an 8½ x 14" (21.5cm x 35.5cm) document and draw crop marks and score marks for a card measuring 4¼" wide (11cm) x 11" (28cm) high. The card will fold in half to a finished size of 4¼" (11cm) wide x 5½" (14cm) high. If your printer is only able to accommodate letter-sized sheets, move your artwork inside the printable aera and print without bleeds.

2 Scan your monogram and floral design and place your artwork inside the crop marks. Allow your floral design to bleed outside the top and bottom of the crops.

3 Print the document on the sheet of white card stock. Use your bone folder to create a centered horizontal score mark. Trim your cards and fold the card on the score mark.

4 Line your envelopes with decorative paper according to the sidebar on page 10.

Flat Card

1 Create an 8½" x 11" (21.5cm x 28cm) document and draw crop marks for 2 flat cards, each measuring 4½" (11.5cm) wide x 5½" (14cm) high.

2 Scan and place your artwork inside the crop marks.

3 Print the document on the sheet of white card stock. Trim your cards to the crop marks.

4 Line your envelopes with decorative paper according to the sidebar on page 10.

CASUAL ENTERTAINING

Dinner Party

Pinwheel-Fold Invitation 32

Guest Sign-In Map 34

Pocket Escort Card 36

Menu 38

Table Marker 40

Soap Label Favor Gift Wrap 41

PARIS, THE MOST POPULAR TOURIST DESTINATION IN THE WORLD, IS FILLED WITH romance, beauty, history, architecture, monuments, jazz, fashion, art museums, and, of course, lovers. My husband proposed to me in Paris, and we honeymooned there. I frequently travel back for long weekends to scour Les Marches aux Puces de Saint-Ouen for antique treasures and flea-market finds that put American ones to shame. The markets are a feast for the senses: the delicious smell of cooking crepes from the street vendor carts, the sound of people conversing quickly in French, the feel of countless textures that you can't help but touch as you pass by.

I may not purchase everything that I fall in love with, but I most definitely take digital photos and mental notes, keeping them in inspirational files for future projects. The paperie for this dinner is one such project. The invitation, guest sign-in, escort cards, table markers, menus, and party favors incorporate so many of the Parisian photographs, artwork, patterns, ephemera, and fonts I have stockpiled over the years.

Your guest list can make or break your dinner party. To avoid an uncomfortable evening, invite people you know won't clash. Six to ten guests is the perfect number; you don't want to spread yourself too thin. As a host of an intimate dinner party, one-on-one personal interaction with each guest is so important. I am a firm advocate of catered dinner parties.

Too often, the host spends the majority of the evening in the kitchen and not enough time enjoying the company of her guests. However, if you love to cook, then I suggest picking dishes that you can mostly prepare before the party and that don't require a huge amount of cleanup.

The Atmosphere

Scatter postcard flipbooks and framed images of famous Parisian monuments: the Eiffel Tower, Arc de Triomphe, Notre Dame Cathedral, Sacré Coeur, and Moulin Rouge. Paint galvanized market buckets in the party's color palette. Fill them with fresh blooms and position them throughout your home. Decorate the bar, coffee table, and counters with secondhand jazz instruments.

Recreate the outdoor café seating prevalent on the Champs Elysees by using small tables—seating two to four guests—covered in sumptuous linens. To promote conversation between tables, group them no more than 2 feet (60cm) apart, and mix couples and single guests. Several glass bud vases holding a single flower create an understated centerpiece. Candles cast a romantic glow over each place setting. Be sure to use scented votives sparingly so that they do not overpower the smell of the food being served. Set the tables the night before your fete. This will reduce stress the day of and give you extra time to attend to last-minute details before the guests arrive.

Paris: Le Franc Pinot on the Ile Saint-Louis. Offer cigars, dim the lights, and play the gypsy jazz of Quintette du Hot Club de France, or the contemporary French jazz of pianist Jean-Michel Pilc while your friends lounge on cozy couches and engage in intimate conversation.

As the evening comes to a close, let everyone wander around and handpick blooms from the market buckets, creating a bouquet of their favorite flowers. Wrap each bouquet in beautiful chartreuse tissue paper and tie it with extra-wide, lavender, double-faced satin ribbon so your guests can enjoy the stems in the days to come.

Hosting Tips

Hire a wandering accordion player to entertain guests with Edith Piaf's "La Vie en Rose" and other French classics. Treat your guests to the atmosphere of one of the best jazz caves in

inspiration boards

At Grapevine, I create "inspiration boards" for clients at the start of every project. It allows them to lay out everything they want me to consider when creating their design. Moving things around and pairing certain items allows me to create a visual palette for my clients and develop the foundation of their design. Afterward, it is a lovely keepsake for the couple to remind them of the start of the creative journey. Once you've chosen a color scheme, theme, and logo or motif,

consider creating an inspiration board incorporating all of the necessary elements of your design. Arrange them in a visually pleasing way. Keep this board on hand for all design decisions. On your quest for the perfect décor, bring your inspiration. Nothing keeps you more focused than a mini version of your party represented on a collage board. Everything from patterns and imagery to ink and fabric swatches are all at your fingertips.

Pinwheel-Fold Invitation

(Makes 1 Invitation)

Photographs, illustrations, French phrases, ornamentation, and a rich collection of fabric patterns found at the Marches add a certain *je ne sais quoi* to this exquisite invitation. Reminiscent of Parisian postcard books from the forties, multiple souvenir cards are wrapped in a lush pinwheel-fold cover. Muted shades of chartreuse and lavender convey the sophistication, warmth, and romance of Paris that awaits them the evening of your soirée.

MATERIALS

- 4 sheets 8½" x 11" (21.5cm x 28cm) white card stock
- 1 sheet 11" x 17" (28cm x 43cm) white card stock
- 5¾" (14.5cm) square chartreuse envelope

TOOLS

- Template and folding guide on page 156
- Craft scissors
- Craft knife, self-healing cutting mat, and ruler
- Bone folder

ARTWORK

- Pattern and frame clipart; photographs of Paris; vintage map of Paris

INSTRUCTIONS

1 Create a 3-page 8½" x 11" (21.5cm x 28cm) document. On each page, draw crop marks for 2 cards that each measure 5" (12.5cm) square. Typeset your text and graphics inside the crop marks. (You will have 6 cards in total. The first card is the invitation, the second card contains the directions, the third is an RSVP, and the final 3 are Paris-inspired collages.) Set type and artwork for the following cards:

- Invitation
- Directions (with map)
- RSVP
- 3 pages with Paris-inspired collages—one for the Eiffel Tower, one for Montmartre, and one for the Moulin Rouge.

2 Print all 3 pages onto 8½" x 11" (21.5cm x 28cm) white card stock. Trim the cards to the crop marks.

3 Create a 2-page 11" x 17" (28cm x 43cm) document. Scan and place the pinwheel-fold template from page 156 on page 1, enlarging it so the overall measurement to the outer edges is 8⅞" (22.5cm) square, and change the color of the template to lavender.

Note: If you do not have a printer that can accommodate 11" x 17" (28cm x 43cm) paper, use a copier to enlarge the template so the overall measurement to the outer edges is 8⅞" (22.5cm). Cut out the template and trace the shape onto decorative or textured paper. Then skip to step 6.

tips

✦ Typeset the wording in French with the translation printed below it. (Free translations are available online.) Ask invitees to check either "Oui!" or "Non!" when returning the RSVP postcard.

✦ Print a map of Paris on the directions card.

4 Place additional artwork in the points of all four corners of the outside frame. Scan and place a floral pattern on page 2 of the document, allowing the pattern to bleed off all 4 edges.

5 Print the template page onto the 11" x 17" (28cm x 43cm) card stock. Flip it over and print the pattern page onto the back of the template.

6 Trim the template side to the edge of the template artwork. Using a bone folder, score and fold where indicated by the folding guide on page 156.

Guest Sign-In Map

(Makes 1 Map with 8 Guest Pins)

Display a vintage map of Paris and entice arrivals to mark their favorite monument, museum, café, arrondissement, or view along the Seine with stickpins bearing their names. The framed map becomes a multidimensional piece of art for your wall and a wonderful reminder of memories shared between friends.

MATERIALS
- Double-sided tape
- 1 package 12" (30.5cm) square cork board tiles (come in packs of 4)
- Map of Paris, to fit in frame and no larger than 24" (61cm) square
- Decorative gilt silver wood frame
- 1 sheet 8½" x 11" (21.5cm x 28cm) white text-weight paper
- 8 Dritz T-Pins size 24 (1½" [3.8cm] long)
- 1 or 2 vintage pincushions

TOOLS
- Craft scissors or craft knife, self-healing cutting mat, and ruler

ARTWORK
- Vintage map of Paris

INSTRUCTIONS

1 Tape the cork tiles to the back of the map. Attach them in a square shape across the entire back of the map with no space between the tiles. Trim the excess cork, and insert the map into the decorative frame.

2 Create an 8½" x 11" (21.5cm x 28cm) document, and draw crop marks for 8 cards, each measuring 1¼" (3cm) wide x 1½" (3.8cm) high to fold in half to 1¼" (3cm) wide x ¾" (2cm) high. Typeset your guests' names.

3 Print the document on the sheet of white text-weight paper. Trim to the crop marks.

4 Fold each name card in half and then open and lay them flat to attach double-sided tape along all four edges on the unprinted side.

5 Place a T-pin onto each card with the crossbar parallel to the fold. Fold the card in half over the top bar of the T-pins and press together.

6 Stick the guest pins into your pincushion and display them in front of the map. Stick your pin with your name on it into the map at your favorite monument or arrondissement so guests can follow your lead.

tips

✦ I created my pincushions using mini French baking tins and foam-stuffed velvet.

✦ Simplify the sign-in process by creating a tented card to display next to the map, explaining what to do.

✦ To display your map, find a frame with an easel back so it can stand on your table on its own, use a floor-standing easel to hold the frame at eye level, or hang it from a beautiful ribbon on your wall.

Pocket Escort Card

(Makes 1 Pocket and 1 Card)

Inspired by the harlequin patterns from vintage art deco posters, these unexpected diamond-shaped escort cards are tucked into adorable V-pocket stands printed with delicate patterns pulled from the invitation design. The cards reveal guests' seating assignments at tables named after *ses monuments*. The perfect beginning for an evening in Paris.

MATERIALS
- 1 sheet 8½" x 11" (21.5cm x 28cm) white card stock
- Double-sided tape

TOOLS
- Template and folding guide on page 157
- Craft scissors or craft knife, self-healing cutting mat, and ruler
- Bone folder

ARTWORK
- Frame clipart on page 157; damask pattern

INSTRUCTIONS

1 Create a 2-page 8½" x 11" (21.5cm x 28 cm) document in your computer page layout or word-processing program. Instead of using crop marks for the pockets and cards, use the Escort Card pocket template and frame clipart on page 157 as a guide for cutting. You will need one pocket and one card per guest, so scan in, enlarging the pocket template to 4⅛" (10.5cm) wide and the frame clipart to 5" (12.5cm) high. Place both the pocket and frame on page 1 of your document.

2 Place a graphic pattern (damask or floral to match the patterns used on your invitation cards) inside the pocket holder frame, letting the pattern bleed over the edges on all 4 sides. Place guest names and seating assignments with artwork inside the card frame. Make page 2 of your document a solid color.

3 Print page 1 of the document on the sheet of white card stock. Turn it over and print page 2 on the back of the sheet. Trim your pocket and seating card just inside the template border. Score and fold the pocket using a bone folder.

4 Place double-sided tape on the flap of the pocket, fold the pocket into place as indicated on the folding guide on page 157, and press down to secure it with the tape.

5 Slip the place card inside so only the guest name is showing. Create one for every guest, and line them up in alphabetical order on a table at the entrance to the festivities.

tips

✦ Alternate patterns and colors on each pocket to add life to your design. Keep in mind that cards will be arranged in alphabetical order by guests' last names, so take that into account when alternating the patterns and colors.

✦ If none of your guests shares the same first name, opt for a more intimate approach, using first names only.

Menu

(Makes 1 Menu)

Share your *joie de vivre* with dinner guests. Prepare a lavish French feast served on your finest china. Present the dinner selections in rich damask-printed folios wrapped in ribbon-laced, silk corsets that echo those worn by cancan dancers at the Moulin Rouge.

MATERIALS

- Spray mount
- 1 sheet of 8½" x 11" (21.5cm x 28cm) lavender card stock
- 8½" x 11" (21.5cm x 28cm) piece lavender silk fabric
- Six ⅛" (3mm) silver eyelets
- 1 sheet 8½" x 11" (21.5cm x 28cm) chartreuse card stock
- 2 sheets 8½" x 11" (21.5cm x 28cm) white card stock
- 18" (45.5cm) lavender ¼"- (6mm-) wide wire-edged organza ribbon
- Double-sided tape

TOOLS

- Bone folder
- Craft knife, self-healing cutting mat, and ruler
- ⅛" (3mm) hole punch
- Eyelet setter with self-healing mat and hammer

ARTWORK

- Pattern clipart

INSTRUCTIONS

1 In a well-ventilated area, spray the adhesive on one side of the lavender card stock and attach it to the lavender silk. Smooth out any wrinkles using a bone folder.

2 Trim the sheet of silk and card stock to 3" x 8½" (7.5cm x 21.5cm). This will remove any thread shags or uneven edges.

3 Punch 3 holes on each end of the strip. The holes should be spaced 1" (2.5cm) apart and ½" (13mm) from the top and bottom edges of the material. Using the eyelet setter with self-healing mat and hammer, set a silver eyelet inside each of the 6 holes.

4 Use a bone folder to score and fold the chartreuse card stock in half to 4¼" (11cm) wide x 11" (28cm) high.

5 Create a 2-page 8½" x 11" (21.5cm x 28cm) document in your computer page layout or word-processing program. Place a graphic pattern (damask or floral to match the patterns used on your invitation cards) on page 1, letting the pattern bleed over the edges on all 4 sides of your page.

6 Print page 1 of the document on a sheet of white card stock. Trim the printed page to 8" (20.5cm) wide x 10½" (26.5cm) high and use a bone folder to score and fold it in half to 4" (10cm) wide x 10½" (26.5cm) high.

7 On page 2 of your document draw crop marks for a card measuring 4" (10cm) wide x 10¾" (27cm) high. Place a pattern inside the crop marks with artwork bleeding off the edges.

Draw a second set of crop marks to the right of the first set for a card measuring 3³⁄₄" (9.5cm) wide x 10¹⁄₂" (26.5cm) high. Typeset your menu text inside the crop marks.

8 Print page 2 of the document on the remaining sheet of white card stock. Trim the patterned and menu cards to the crop marks.

9 Using double-sided tape, attach the menu card to the center of the patterned card. Then attach the patterned card to the center of the inside right-hand panel of your folded chartreuse card (from step 4).

10 Fold the chartreuse card closed and wrap the folded patterned card (from step 7) around the outside, leaving an even ¹⁄₄" (6mm) border along the top, right, and bottom edges.

11 Fold the sheet of silk and card stock around the outside of both the chartreuse and patterned card, positioning the eyelet edges along the long edges of the card. Lace the ribbon through the eyelets and finish with a petite bow. Curl the ends of the ribbon for a less buttoned-up look.

Table Marker

(Makes 1 Table Marker)

Paris comes to life in these exquisite table markers. Rather than the predictable table number or name, images of famous landmarks welcome guests to their tables, making a sophisticated statement and blending seamlessly with table décor.

MATERIALS
- 1 sheet 8½" x 11" (21.5cm x 28cm) lavender card stock
- 1 sticker of a Paris site

TOOLS
- Craft knife, self-healing cutting mat, and ruler
- Bone folder

ARTWORK
- Eiffel Tower postcard sticker; Cavalini Paris stickers in a tin

INSTRUCTIONS

1 Trim the lavender card stock to ½" (13mm) larger than your sticker in height and width when the card stock is folded in half. For instance, if your sticker is 3" x 5" (7.5cm x 12.5cm), your lavender card stock should be 3½" x 11" (9cm x 28cm), which folds to 3½" x 5½" (9cm x 14cm).

2 Use a bone folder to score and fold in half.

3 Peel off the backing and place the sticker in the center of one side of the folded card.

tips

✦ Vintage postcards and illustrations of Paris, adhered with double-sided tape, are a great alternative to the stickers.

✦ Use the same Paris frame for each table marker, but alternate the landmark image at every table.

Soap Label Favor Gift Wrap

(Makes 1 Sheet of Gift Wrap)

Give the gift of indulgence. Delicious verbena and cucumber scented French-milled soaps are packaged in vintage-style soap label wrapping paper. Personalize the label with your party information and alter the patterns and colors to create a gorgeous gift display.

MATERIALS
- 1 bar French-milled soap
- 1 sheet 8½" x 11" (21.5cm x 28cm) white text-weight paper
- Gift tape or Scotch tape

TOOLS
- Ruler
- Craft knife, self-healing cutting mat, and ruler

ARTWORK
- Pattern and frame clipart

INSTRUCTIONS

1 Measure your soap bar, taking into account the size of the front, sides, and back plus an overlap of about ½" (13mm) for taping the gift wrap. Create an 8½" x 11" (21.5cm x 28cm) document in your computer page layout or word-processing program and draw crop marks to fit the measurements.

2 Scan your pattern and frame art and place your artwork centered inside the crop marks. Typeset the text, including the soap name/fragrance, date, and your name.

3 Print the document on the sheet of white card stock. Trim your wrapper to the crop marks.

4 Wrap around your soap bar, and use tape to secure as you would a gift package.

tips

✦ Alternate between lavender and chartreuse for patterns and fonts, and alternate the colors when stacking them on your display table.

✦ For the most luxuriant French-milled soaps, visit FrenchSoaps.com or Lothantique.com.

Outdoor Fete

Scroll Invitation 44

Signature Drink Sign and Tag 46

Utensil Display 48

Menu Paddle Fan. 51

Bread Bag Favor Tag 52

WHETHER YOU THROW AN INTIMATE BACKYARD GET-TOGETHER OR A LAVISH outdoor gathering, what better way is there to kick off summer's long hot days and cool evenings than with a summer solstice celebration? You can't help but smile and think of summer when you look at this lively color palette of lemon yellow and lime green. Wedges, slices, and whole fruits are combined in playful ways, adding an abundance of cheer to your paperie and décor.

The Atmosphere

The beauty of an outdoor setting is really all you need, but a few touches here and there, mirroring your paperie design, will truly personalize your gathering. If entertaining in the heat of the day, create shady retreats under raw fabric panels stretched between trees with clothesline and grommets. Form seating areas under these cool spots for guests to escape the hot sunrays. There is no better excuse for lounging in the afternoon breeze than a comfy cushioned chair or chaise!

Then, as the sun goes down, consider extending your home to the patio. Create an outdoor living space complete with a table, couches, chairs, a full bar, a fire pit, a grill, and even lamps. Set a stylish table using colorful fabric runners in dots and stripes. Cut them with pinking shears to create a rickrack edge, and top them with clear glass plates so your guests can see the fabric underneath. Scatter potted hydrangea and white milk glass bowls filled with fresh lemons and limes on picnic tables, countertops, and side tables to carry the paperie theme throughout your party setting in a natural yet refined way.

Hosting Tips

For entertainment, croquet and horseshoes during the day are a must. Both create some healthy competition and fun conversation among guests without their working up a sweat or getting dirty. Try a themed piñata or pull out the childhood board games.

For nostalgic fun, toast marshmallows and catch fireflies when the sun goes down. I don't care how old you are—sparklers are irresistible! Tie them in bundles with pretty ribbon and matches, and stand them up in citrus-colored pails filled with sand.

Mr. Robert Cummings
122 WEST 28TH STREET
NUMBER 18B
NEW YORK CITY
1 0 0 0 1

··· COME CELEBRATE ···

THE
Summer
SOLSTICE

·· AND JOIN US FOR ··

A Little Slice of Paradise

Saturday, the twenty-first of June
FROM NOON
UNTIL SIX O'CLOCK

At Our Home

Kristen and Michael Harrison

6 TUCKER ROAD
BRAINTREE, MASSACHUSETTS

KINDLY R.S.V.P.
BY THE FIRST OF JUNE
781·843·99

Scroll Invitation

(Makes 1 Invitation)

Announce your decadent summer solstice celebration with a dramatic yet unpretentious invitation scroll, finished with a delicate lemon-yellow gingham-checked ribbon and presented in a box on a lush bed of bright-green tissue grass.

MATERIALS

- Four 1" (2.5cm) wood dowel caps with ⅜" (9.5mm) hole
- White acrylic paint (gloss)
- 1 sheet 15" x 30" (38cm x 76cm) green tissue-paper grass mat
- 1 gift box 5" x 7" x 1" (12.5cm x 18cm x 2.5cm) kraft paper-covered
- 1 sheet 11" x 17" (28cm x 43cm) white text-weight paper
- 1 sheet 11" x 17" (28cm x 43cm) white crack-and-peel label stock
- Two 7"- (18cm-) long dowel rods, ⅜" (9.5mm) diameter
- One 12" piece of ½"- (13mm-) wide yellow gingham-check wire-edged ribbon

TOOLS

- ½"- (13mm-) wide foam paintbrush
- Craft scissors
- Hot-glue gun
- Craft knife, self-healing cutting mat, and ruler

ARTWORK

- Citrus clipart; decorative frame clipart

INSTRUCTIONS

1 Paint the 4 dowel caps with white acrylic paint and set aside to dry.

2 Cut a piece of green tissue-paper grass mat to 5" x 7" (12.5cm x 18cm), and use hot glue to affix it inside the bottom of the kraft paper-covered box.

3 Trim the sheet of 11" x 17" (28cm x 43cm) paper to 8½" x 17" (21.5cm x 43cm). Trim the crack-and-peel label stock to 8½" x 17" (21.5cm x 43cm).

4 Create a 2-page document in your computer page layout or word-processing program with each page 5½" (14cm) wide x 16" (40.64cm) high for the back and front of the invitation scroll. Draw a solid frame with edges around the entire document to ensure accurate cutting. If you are using a page layout program, skip this step and just be sure to print your layout with crop marks. On page 1 of your scroll document, typeset using the photograph as a guide. On page 2, lay out your citrus graphics.

5 Print page 1 of the document on the white text-weight paper. Flip the paper over and print page 2 (the citrus pattern) on the back of the scroll. Trim only the left and right sides of your scroll to the border or crop marks. You will need the full 17" (21.5cm) length to wrap around your scroll rods. When you roll and glue the scroll ends around the rod, the frame edge or crop marks at the ends of the scroll will be hidden.

6 For the mailing label, create a document in your computer page layout or word-processing program that is 6¾" (17cm) wide x 13" (33cm) high. Draw a solid frame around the entire document to ensure accurate cutting. If you

are using a page layout program, skip this step and just be sure to print your layout with crop marks. Lay out your type.

7 Print the document on the white crack-and-peel label stock. Trim your mailing label to the border or crop marks.

8 When your dowel caps are dry, hot-glue one to each end of each dowel rod. You now have 2 complete scroll rods.

9 Run a bead of hot glue along the 5½" (14cm) end of the paper scroll about ⅛" (3mm) in from the edge on the invitation side (not the citrus side). Quickly attach it to the first scroll rod before the glue cools and hardens. Run a second parallel bead of hot glue 1" (2.5cm) down from the first bead and wrap the paper scroll around the scroll rod until you pass the glue bead. Hold

in place until the glue cools. This will ensure that the paper covers the dowel of the scroll rod entirely. Repeat this for the other 5½" (14cm) end of the scroll, using the second scroll rod.

10 When the glue is cool, roll the two ends of paper scroll around the scroll rods until the rods meet in the center of the paper scroll. Tie yellow gingham-check ribbon in a bow around the dowel rods to keep the scroll from unrolling. Place the scroll inside the box on the bed of tissue paper, and close the lid.

11 Remove the protective backing from the mailing label and wrap it around the entire box to seal it for safe mailing.

more hosting tips

✦ Guests expect paper napkins at an outdoor gathering. Instead, add a touch of comfort and color to your refreshment spread by offering disposable cloth napkins. Purchase inexpensive color-coordinated fabrics and cut them into large squares using pinking shears. Roll them and display them in an open wire basket. They will instantly become part of the décor.

✦ For an unexpected treat, I once tipped off our local ice cream man about our summer party. As requested, he drove by at the stroke of 7 pm with music playing, to the delight of all of our guests. I couldn't hold back the laughter watching our adult friends and family scrambling for money and running out to the front yard for dessert. The photos are priceless!

✦ Set up an "outdoor essentials" buffet consisting of sunscreen, antibacterial and bug-repellant wet-wipes, and mints displayed in pretty bowls so guests can help themselves.

Signature Drink Sign and Tag

(Makes 1 Drink Jug Sign and 15 Canning Jar Tags)

Both fun and functional, half-pint Ball® canning jars with glass covers rimmed with beaded silver wire and decorated with pretty "Drink in the Sunshine!" tags are the perfect container for a signature citrus drink. The jar covers prevent flying critters and pollen from "garnishing" your guests' cocktails.

MATERIALS

- 1 sheet 8½" x 11" (21.5cm x 28cm) white card stock
- Double-sided tape
- 150 lime-green glass seed beads
- 150 yellow glass seed beads
- 7½ yd (6.9m) 22-gauge bright silver floral/craft wire

TOOLS

- Craft scissors
- Craft knife, self-healing cutting mat, and ruler
- Corner rounder
- ⅛" (3mm) hole punch

ARTWORK

- Citrus clipart; decorative frame clipart

INSTRUCTIONS

1 Create an 8½" x 11" (21.5cm x 28cm) document in your computer page layout or word-processing program and draw crop marks for the sign for the front of your drink jug. (The sign featured here measures 4¾" x 2¾" [12cm x 7cm].) On the same page, create fifteen 2¼" x 1¼" (5.5cm x 3cm) tags for the front of your canning jars. Instead of using crop marks, set frame around the text. Set your type and graphics for the sign and tags.

2 Print the document on the sheet of white card stock. Trim your jug sign to the crop marks and attach your sign to the front of the jug with double-sided tape.

3 Trim the jar tags, leaving a ⅛" (3mm) border of white space around the edge of each frame.

4 Punch holes on the left- and right-hand sides of each drink jar tag just inside the frame.

5 Cut the bright silver floral/craft wire into fifteen 18" (45.5cm) lengths, and string each with 9 green and 9 yellow beads, alternating the colors as you string them.

6 Wrap the beaded wire creatively around the neck of your canning jar, and thread the two ends through the ⅛" (3mm) holes at each side of the drink jar tag.

7 Add one more bead to each wire end and finish by twisting the wire tips around the end beads until they are secure. This will ensure that the other beads will not slide off the ends of the wire.

Utensil Display

(Makes 3 Signs)

Who says plastic picnic ware has to be boring? Purchase colorful utensils and create an attractive display by standing them up in square glass vases filled with dried split peas. As guests take their forks, knives, and spoons, the peas fill in the empty space and keep the remaining utensils from falling over.

MATERIALS
- 3 sheets 8½" x 11" (21.5cm x 28cm) white crack-and-peel label stock
- 3 square glass vases
- 9 bags of dried split peas

TOOLS
- Craft knife, self-healing cutting mat, and ruler

ARTWORK
- Citrus clipart; decorative frame clipart; computer-drawn stripes

INSTRUCTIONS

1 Create a document with 3 pages in your computer page layout or word-processing program setting crop marks for the signs on the front of your vases. (I used a 6" x 4" x 6" [15cm x 10cm x 15cm] deep vase, so my signs were 4" x 7" [10cm x 18cm]; adjust the size of your signs to fit the vases you choose allowing for overlap.) Set your type and graphics—forks, spoons, knives—for each sign. Lay out one sign per page in your document.

2 Print the document on the three sheets of white crack-and-peel label stock. Trim the signs to the crop marks.

3 Peel off the protective backing on each sign and attach your signs to the front of each vase, wrapping the signs over the top to bottom edges of the vases.

4 Fill each vase with 3 bags of split peas and arrange your utensils.

tip

✦ When filling the vases with peas, leave about ½" (13mm) of space at the top of the vase (as you would with flowers and water). Your utensils will take up room in the vase and cause the peas to rise as you add utensils.

Menu Paddle Fan

(Makes 1 Fan)

In the warm summer months, these menus are sure to be appreciated by every guest. Dinner selections double as paddle fans and are perfect outdoors, where air conditioning is unavailable.

MATERIALS
- 2 sheets 8½" x 11" (21.5cm x 28cm) white card stock
- Double-sided tape
- 1 unfinished wood jumbo Popsicle stick

TOOLS
- Craft knife, self-healing cutting mat, and ruler
- Corner rounding punch
- Hot-glue gun

ARTWORK
- Citrus clipart; decorative frame clipart; computer-drawn stripes

INSTRUCTIONS

1 Create an 8½" x 11" (21.5cm x 28cm) document in your computer page layout or word-processing program and draw crop marks for a card measuring 6" (15cm) wide x 6½" (16.5cm) high. Design the card with yellow and green stripes of varying widths or a pattern of lemons and limes.

2 Create a second page in your document and draw crop marks for the menu measuring 5" (12.5cm) wide x 5½" (14cm) high. Set text and graphics for the menu inside the crops.

3 Print each page on a sheet of white card stock. Trim both to the crop marks. Use your corner rounding punch to round all four corners of both cards.

4 With the printing on both cards facing you, attach the menu card to the front of the larger patterned card with double-sided tape. Be sure to make the space between the edges of the cards even on all 4 sides.

5 Glue the jumbo Popsicle stick to the center of the back of the larger card using your hot-glue gun.

tips

✦ A worn, white wire basket adds a light, airy feel to your display and allows guests to see the basket contents from a distance. Or, place a fan at each place setting to add to the table décor.

✦ Additional layers of card stock will create a sturdier, more luxurious fan.

Bread Bag Favor Tag

(Makes 8 Favor Tags)

Make your sweets look even sweeter. Bundle color-coordinated candies in white scrim, and cinch the top with an inventive "bread bag" favor tag. Display them on white milk glass pedestals or compotes in varying heights.

MATERIALS
- 1 sheet 8½" x 11" (21.5cm x 28cm) white card stock
- ¼ yd (23cm) of 56"- (142cm-) wide white netting, scrim, or sheer fabric
- Selection of sweets

TOOLS
- Template on page 159
- ¼" (6mm) hole punch
- Craft scissors or craft knife, self-healing cutting mat, and ruler
- Corner rounding punch

ARTWORK
- Decorative swirl clipart

INSTRUCTIONS

1 Create a document in your computer page layout or word-processing program that is 8½" (21.5cm) wide x 11" (28cm) high. Draw eight 1½" (3.8cm) wide x 3 1⁄10" (7.9cm) high green rectangles on the page or use the Bread Bag Favor Tag template on page 159, enlarged to the dimensions above. Place your favor tag message inside the squares using white text.

2 Print the document on the sheet of white card stock. Trim the tags. Use your corner rounding punch to round all corners of the cards.

3 Use the Bread Bag Favor Tag template on page 159 as a guide to punch a hole in the horizontal center of the card and cut a slice from the center of the hole to the top edge of the card.

4 Cut the netting into eight 6" (15cm) circles and fill with sweets.

5 Wrap the sweets with netting, gathering the edges at the top central point. Twist the top of your netting until it is tight and slide it through the slice of the favor tag until the netting twist rests in the center of the favor tag hole, just as you would secure a bag of bread with a plastic tab.

Wine Tasting

Gate-Fold Invitation 57

Reminder Postcard 57

Tasting Note 60

Blind Tasting Bottle Cover 62

Wine-Tasting Program Kiosk 64

Wine-Glass Tag 65

Drink Coaster 66

INVITE YOUR FRIENDS TO "SAVOR A YEAR FULL OF FLAVOR" AND PLAN MULTIPLE wine tastings throughout the coming year. Each tasting should feature wines from different regions around the world that pique palates and transport guests to faraway places. These tastings are not about soliciting a professional opinion or developing an expert palate. They are about discovering your personal likes and dislikes while enjoying great wine with close friends. Whether you make the evening formal by hiring a certified sommelier to guide and pour or put a more casual spin on the night and simply rate wines and discover new favorites, these paperie projects—invitation, bottle covers, tasting notes, program kiosk, reminder postcards, coasters, and glass tags—as well as the tips in this chapter are your formula for success.

Choose Your Wine

A wine-tasting "flight" is a selection of three to eight wines for you to sample, examine, assess, compare, rate and/or judge. Hold a "vertical tasting" by selecting different vintages of the same wine type from the same winery, or a "horizontal tasting" by sampling wines with the same vintage from different wineries. Choosing wines by variety, type, and region emphasizes their unique characteristics.

Basic wine tasting parties are a breeze to plan: Just serve light hors d'oeuvres before the tasting begins or pair your wine selections with cheese and dessert. Hosting a more complex "pairings" dinner requires additional planning and foresight. Choose four to six bottles, pairing them horizontally or vertically. Use a pairing wheel (available at Turning leaf.com) to determine which foods each wine will complement. Budget a half bottle per guest every three hours. Serve a taste of each wine with a single food dish. Guests will marvel at how various wines interact with the same food and how some wines can actually change the way the food tastes! Pairings are extremely subjective, so the wheel should be used as a general guideline to give you ideas from Chinese food to chocolate.

YOU ARE INVITED TO SAVOR
A YEAR FULL OF FLAVOR
AND TOAST THE GOOD LIFE

WITH

HANNA FALLON

BEGINNING WITH
A SELECTION

OF

Petit Sirah

CHICAGO, ILLINOIS

2008

R.S.V.P. TO (312) 266-7997 BY JANUARY SECOND

PRODUCED BY HANNA FALLON
661 NORTH STATE STREET

7:00 pm

Jan.15

VINTAGE 2008

661 NORTH STATE STREET
CHICAGO, ILLINOIS
60610

Another take on a traditional wine tasting is to host a *Sideways* movie tasting. Play the film's soundtrack and sample wines consumed throughout the movie:

- 1961 Chateau Cheval Blanc
- 1988 Tenuta San Guido Sassicaia
- 1992 Byron Santa Maria Valley Brut Reserve
- 1995 Opus One
- 1998 Dominique Laurent Pommard
- 2001 Fiddlehead Happy Canyon Sauvignon Blanc
- 2001 Hitching Post Pinot Noir
- 2001 Kistler Camp Meeting Ridge Chardonnay
- 2001 Sanford Pinot Noir, Chardonnay, and Vin Gris
- 2002 Andrew Murray Cellars Syrah
- 2002 Melville Vineyards Pinot Noir
- 2002 Sea Smoke Cellars Botella Pinot Noir
- 2002 Talley Pinot Noir Estate
- 2002 Tantara Pinot Noir

I regularly join friends to enjoy great bottles of red wine at our homes and attend formal wine tastings at Les Zygomates in Boston. I have my special-occasion favorites and my everyday go-to wines, but every year I still purchase *The Essential Wine Buying Guide* to find and review recommended vintages. I would suggest purchasing the guide, published every year by the Wine Enthusiast. It offers up-to-date information on more than 40,000 wines. Another great resource is the *Pocket Wine Book* by the United Kingdom's top wine critic, Hugh Johnson.

The Atmosphere

Keep decorations to a minimum. Recreate the atmosphere of your favorite local wine bar or restaurant by covering the tasting table with either butcher paper or a white tablecloth. Accent it with a few simple floral arrangements flanked by tall taper candles.

Plan the music ahead of time: For a wine tasting with a "Taste of Tuscany" theme, play the ever-popular Italian singer/songwriter Lucio Battisti. If you plan to serve Spanish wines, play mariachi music. Tasting reds? Strum up a little bluegrass by Red Wine.

Hosting Tips

Prime the palates by prominently displaying a tasting wheel. I suggest the Beringer wine tasting wheel (available at Beringer.com), which breaks out red and white wines. It is a valuable learning tool and offers a comprehensive list of descriptive terms that can be used to accurately describe the wines.

To get started, pour approximately two ounces of wine in each glass. Ask your guests to smell the wine before tasting it to detect the elements in the "nose" of the wine. Instruct them to swirl the wine in their glasses and then inhale the aroma. To help identify the elements, inhale ingredients, such as cherries, licorice, and cedar, listed in the vineyard's tasting notes for each wine.

After sipping, read the tasting notes and discuss, reflecting on the subtle nuances of each flavor. Everyone should then write their descriptions and notes on appearance, aroma, flavor, and finish on the custom tasting cards provided.

Tasters should pour any leftover wine from their glasses into the buckets provided and swirl water in them before the next selection is served. Between tastes, your guests should inhale the scent of fresh coffee grounds (provided in small bowls) to clear their noses. Encourage them to nibble on mild cheese, crackers, or bread to further cleanse their palates between wines.

End the evening with chocolates or cheesecake paired with a dessert wine and bid your guests farewell with a promise to see them at the next tasting. Cheers!

More than 75 percent of what we taste is determined by our sense of smell. Our tongue senses four basic tastes: sweet, sour, bitter, and salty (and recently a fifth basic taste, called *umami*, for savory, non-salty flavors, has been acknowledged). But these have little to do with our sensory perception of wine: It is our nose that sends the major signals to the brain about the bouquet and flavor of the wine we are drinking.

Gate-Fold Invitation and Reminder Postcard

(Makes 1 Invitation and 2 Postcards)

Announce the year of tastings with a deluxe orange-and-gray wine-label invitation wrapped in natural cork paper backed with brilliant orange lokta (rice paper) and sealed with copper wax. (Invitation is shown on page 55 and Reminder Postcard is shown on page 59.)

MATERIALS

Invitation

- 1 sheet 8½" x 11" (21.5cm x 28cm) white card stock
- Spray mount
- 1 sheet 8½" x 11" (21.5cm x 28cm) cork paper
- 1 sheet 8½" x 11" (21.5cm x 28cm) orange textured paper (I used lokta paper)
- 1 sheet 8½" x 11" (21.5cm x 28cm) gray card stock
- Double-sided tape

- 2 yd (1.8m) orange or brown bookbinder's waxed thread
- 2 copper-colored sealing wax sticks
- 1 sheet 8½" x 11" (21.5cm x 28cm) white crack-and-peel label
- 1 gray A7 (5¼" x 7¼" [13.3cm x 18.5cm]) envelope (I used Paper Source's Cement envelope)

Reminder Postcard

- 1 sheet 8½" x 11" (21.5cm x 28cm) white card stock
- 1 sheet 8½" x 11" (21.5cm x 28cm) cork paper

TOOLS

- Craft knife, self-healing cutting mat, and ruler
- Bone folder
- 2 clothespins
- Hot-glue gun
- Wax seal with your first or last initial

ARTWORK

- Crown and vintage ornamental rules clipart; orange frame around the invitation and label are standard picture-box frames found in my layout program (I use Quark Xpress).

INSTRUCTIONS

Invitation

1 Create an 8½" x 11" (21.5cm x 28cm) document in your computer page layout or word-processing program and draw crop marks for your invitation card. The card should be 4½" (11.5cm) wide x 6⅕" (16.5cm) high.

2 Place your scanned artwork and set the type for the invitation card, using your own chosen wine label or the photograph on page 55 as a guide. Include the type of wine guests will sample along with the celebration details.

3 Print the document on the sheet of white card stock. Trim your card to the crop marks.

4 In a well-ventilated area, spray adhesive on the back of the cork sheet and attach it to the sheet of orange paper. This will add visual interest and weight to your cover.

5 Trim the cover (the cork and orange paper) to 10¼" x 7" (26cm x 18cm). Use your bone folder to fold the center panel of the cover to 5" x 7" (12.5cm x 18cm), by folding a 2½" x 7" (6.5cm x 18cm) left-hand panel and a 2¾" x 7" (7cm x 18cm) right-hand panel. There will be a ¼" (6mm) overlap when you close your cover.

6 Using double-sided tape, attach the trimmed invitation card to the gray card stock to create a second layer. Trim the gray card stock, leaving ⅛" (3mm) on all 4 sides.

7 Attach the layered invitation card to the center of the inside panel of your cover using double-sided tape.

8 Fold the cover closed. Use the clothespins to hold each panel closed while you wrap the bookbinder's thread horizontally around the cover a few times in an interesting criss-cross pattern and tie it in a knot over the right-hand panel. Remove the clothespins after you tie the knot.

9 Heat the wax sticks in the hot-glue gun. (You will need 2 sticks to fill the glue chamber, but each wax stick will yield 5-10 seals depending on the amount of wax you use for each seal.) Squeeze wax onto the knot you tied in the bookbinder's thread and press your initial wax seal into the wax. Hold for approximately 15 seconds or until wax cools and hardens slightly. Carefully remove the wax seal from your wax and set it aside to cool. Do not touch the wax for at least 5 minutes, as your fingerprints will transfer into the wax before it cools completely.

10 For your envelope label, create an 8½" x 11" (21.5cm x 28cm) document in your computer page layout or word-processing program and draw crop marks measuring 1" (2.5cm) wide x 7½" (19cm) high. It will fold in half to 1" (2.5cm) wide x 3¾" (9.5cm) high. Set your crown, vintage rules, and type inside the crop marks on the lower half of the return address label. Copy and paste the artwork, rotate it 180 degrees, and set it inside the crop marks on the other half of the address label.

11 Print the label on the sheet of white crack-and-peel label stock. Trim to crop marks. Peel off the protective backing and fold the address label over the top of your sealed envelope to mimic the neck of a wine bottle. Press down to keep it in place.

tip

✦ Since the end of the return address label extends beyond the edge of the envelope flap, be sure to address your envelope, insert your invitation, and seal the envelope before applying your return address label.

Reminder Postcard

1 Create an 8½" x 11" (21.5cm x 28cm) document and draw crop marks for 2 flat cards, each measuring 5" (12.5cm) wide x 7" (18cm) high.

2 Scan your crown and decorative rules and place your artwork and text inside the crop marks. Include the date, time, RSVP instructions, and wine selection for the upcoming tasting on the left-hand side and the guests' names and addresses on the right-hand side.

3 Print the document on the sheet of white card stock. Spray adhesive on the unprinted side of your card stock and press it onto the back side of the cork paper. Your postcard will be covered in cork on one side and have the information and mailing address on the other.

4 Trim your cards to the crop marks.

what you need for a basic tasting

- Six to twelve friends
- Appetizers for before or after
- Four to six wines (the standard pour is 2 to 2½ ounces, which is approximately 10 tastes per bottle)
- A bottle opener with foil cutter
- A decanter for red wine (aerating wine with a decanter softens harsh tannins and separates the sediment to ensure optimal bouquet and taste, but this is optional!)

- Buckets of ice to chill white wine or champagne bottles
- Wine glasses (one per guest)
- Water, mild cheeses, bread, and crackers to cleanse the palate between wines
- Coffee grounds to neutralize the nose after each wine
- Pitchers of water for rinsing glasses when changing wines
- Buckets for discarding wine and water between pourings

- Tasting note cards and pens for guests to record and rate the wines tasted
- Blind tasting wine covers
- Good conversation (encourage guests to share their thoughts and reactions to each wine)

For ideas on how to host more than thirty different wine tastings, read the Wine Enthusiast's *Pocket Guide to Wine* (available at WineEnthusiast.com).

Tasting Note

(Makes 1 Tasting Note)

Tasting notes allow attendees to keep track of the tasting and refer to their own notes later when purchasing their favorites from the evening's selections. Highlight the party's location with a vintage map of your city and embellish the folded tasting notes with a decorative belly band. Distribute them with matching pens before the tasting begins.

MATERIALS
- 2 sheets 8½" x 11" (21.5cm x 28cm) white text-weight paper
- Decorative pen

TOOLS
- Craft knife, self-healing cutting mat, and ruler
- Double-sided tape

ARTWORK
- Vintage map

INSTRUCTIONS

1 Create a 2-page 8½" x 11" (21.5cm x 28cm) document in your computer page layout or word-processing program. Place your scanned map on page 1 of the document. Be sure to leave a ½" (13mm) border all the way around the map to ensure that your map is inside the printable area of your inkjet or laser printer.

2 Typeset your tasting notes on the second page. Each of the quadrants on your page should have space for the wine name, vintage and grape variety, producer, region, color/appearance, nose/aroma, mouth/flavor, conclusions/impressions, food pairings, price (bottle/case), and alcohol content.

3 Print the map page of the document on a sheet of white text-weight paper. Turn the page over and print the tasting notes on the back side of the map. Trim the unprinted border off the map side of your sheet.

4 Fold the tasting notes into quarters (fold in half and then in half again) so that the final folded size is 3¾" x 5" (9.5cm x 12.5cm), with the map side facing out.

5 Create another 8½" x 11" (21.5cm x 28cm) document for the tasting notes belly band. Draw crop marks for a strip of paper measuring ½" (13mm) high x 9½" (24cm) wide. Set your type with "Tasting Notes" and the date of the tasting surrounded by a simple decorative border.

6 Print on a sheet of white text-weight paper. Trim your belly bands to the crop marks.

7 Wrap the belly band around the folded tasting notes sheet, making sure to center the text on the front panel. Secure with double-sided tape on the tail ends of the band on the back of the tasting notes.

Blind Tasting Bottle Cover

(Makes 1 Bottle Cover)

Slip bottles into numbered cork paper sleeves to cover the labels of each wine, eliminating prejudices at the start of the tasting. Line the bottles up at the head of the tasting table with tasting notes for each bottle. Even if no one correctly identifies the wine, the game will trigger conversation and interaction among guests and add an element of surprise.

MATERIALS
- 1 sheet 8½" x 11" (21.5cm x 28cm) white crack-and-peel label
- 1 sheet 8½" x 11" (21.5cm x 28cm) cork paper
- Double-sided tape

TOOLS
- Craft knife, self-healing cutting mat, and ruler

INSTRUCTIONS

1 Create an 8½" x 11" [21.5cm x 28cm] document in your computer page layout or word-processing program. Draw crop marks for a card measuring 3¼" (8.3cm) wide x 4½" (11.5cm) high. (If you are covering multiple bottles, 4 labels can fit on one 8½" x 11" [21.5cm x 28cm] label sheet.)

2. Place the bottle number and a simple frame inside your borders or crops. Set your card's background to orange, and reverse the color of the type and frame to white.

3 Print on the white crack-and-peel label. Trim the document to the crop marks.

4 Measure your wine bottle. (Though wine bottles hold the same volume, the circumference and height of the bottles can vary slightly.) Cut a strip of the cork paper to cover the label of your wine bottle for blind tastings, adding a ½" (13mm) overlap. Wrap the cork around the entire bottle, and secure the ends of the cork to each other with double-sided tape.

5 Remove the protective backing on the printed crack-and-peel label and place your number in the center of the cork paper on the front of the wine bottle.

tips

✦ Begin your wine tasting with an informational lesson about the grape or region you are sampling. Include geography, traditions, history, and climate.

✦ An average wine tasting samples 3-4 bottles of wine.

✦ Don't attach the labels directly to the bottle—make sure they can easily be removed to reveal wines after tasting concludes. This will allow guests to accurately record the wines for future purchase.

Wine-Tasting Program Kiosk

(Makes 1 Kiosk)

Place multiple card stock kiosks around the room featuring the dates and wines for the year's tasting schedule. Include famous quotes about wine such as "Wine is bottled poetry" by Robert Louis Stevenson, "If God forbade drinking, would he have made wine so good?" by Cardinal Richelieu, and "From wine what sudden friendship springs!" by John Gay.

MATERIALS
- 2 sheets 8½" x 11" (21.5cm x 28cm) white card stock
- Double-sided tape

TOOLS
- Craft knife, self-healing cutting mat, and ruler
- Bone folder

ARTWORK
- Crown and vintage ornamental rules clipart

INSTRUCTIONS

1 Create an 8" (20.5cm) wide x 10½" (26.5cm) high document in your computer page layout or word-processing program. Draw crop marks or a solid frame around the entire document to ensure accurate cutting. If you are using a page layout program, skip this step and just be sure to print your layout with crop marks. Also place vertical crop marks at 3¾" (9.5cm) and 7½" (19cm) across the page to indicate where to score for the card's folds.

2 Scan crown and decorative rule artwork. Place your artwork and text inside the frame or crop marks on the two 3¾"- (9.5cm-) wide panels. The ½" (13mm) panel on the right-hand side of the printed document will be used as a tape flap to create your four-panel kiosk. Be sure to include all wine tasting dates and themes for the coming year on one panel and quotes or poems about wine/drinking on the second panel.

3 Print 2 copies of the document on the white card stock. Before trimming, use the point of your bone folder and a ruler to score the folds at 3¾" (9.5cm) and 7½" (19cm). Trim the document to the border or crop marks. Use your bone folder to fold each page on the score marks.

4 Attach the 2 folded cards together by placing double-sided tape along the entire length of each ½"- (13mm-) wide end flap and pressing each end flap onto the inside edge of the 3¾"- (9.5cm-) wide panel of the opposite card, creating a four-sided free-standing kiosk.

Wine-Glass Tag

(Makes 10 Tags)

When serving the remaining bottles of wine with other refreshments at the conclusion of each tasting, distribute fresh glasses tagged with guests' names. This tiny decorative accessory will be invaluable, preventing glasses from getting misplaced or mixed up throughout the evening.

MATERIALS
- 1 sheet 8½" x 11" (21.5cm x 28cm) white card stock
- 2 sheets 9" x 12" (23cm x 30.5cm) Avery self-adhesive laminating sheets
- 10 copper or silver eyelets
- Ten 4"- (10cm-) long nickel-plated ball chain keychains
- ⅛" (3mm) hole punch
- Eyelet setter, hammer, and self-healing mat

TOOLS
- Craft knife, self-healing cutting mat, and ruler

ARTWORK
- Crown and vintage ornamental rules clipart

INSTRUCTIONS

1 Create an 8½" x 11" (21.5cm x 28cm) document in your computer page layout or word-processing program and draw crop marks for 10 wine-glass tags that each measure ¾" (2cm) high x 1½" (3.8cm) wide. Place a simple frame inside the crop marks. Typeset each guest's name inside the frames of the tags.

2 Print the document on the sheet of white card stock. Peel off the backing of the Avery self-adhesive laminating sheets and press one onto each side of the card stock, following the enclosed Avery instructions. Trim your laminated sheet of tags to the crop marks.

3 Punch a single hole in the left-hand side of each tag. Using your hammer, eyelet setter, and self-healing mat, set the copper eyelets in the holes to reinforce them.

4 Thread one ball chain through each eyelet hole and attach to the stem of a wine glass.

Drink Coaster

(Makes 2 Coasters)

Scatter stylish cork-backed coasters, emblazoned with your crown logo and a vintage map of your city, throughout the party. Functional yet refined, they will continue your theme while saving your countertops and tables from permanent drink stains.

MATERIALS
- 1 sheet 8½" x 11" (21.5cm x 28cm) white card stock
- 1 sheet 9" x 12" (23cm x 30.5cm) Avery® self-adhesive laminating sheets (sold in packs of 50 sheets)
- 1 sheet 12" (30.5cm) square cork board tile (come in packs of 4)

TOOLS
- Craft knife, self-healing cutting mat, and ruler
- Hot-glue gun

ARTWORK
- Crown clipart; vintage map

INSTRUCTIONS

1 Create an 8½" x 11" (21.5cm x 28cm) document in your computer page layout or word-processing program and draw crop marks for your 2 coaster cards. Each card should be 3¾" (9.5cm) square. Place your scanned art inside your crop marks.

2 Print the document on the sheet of white card stock. Peel off the protective backing of the Avery self-adhesive laminating sheet and press onto the printed side of the card stock only, following the enclosed Avery instructions. Trim the laminated card to the crop marks.

3 Hot glue each coaster card to the cork board tile with your hot-glue gun.

4 Trim the cork tile around the coaster card, leaving a ⅛" (3mm) border on each side of the card.

The rule of thumb for filling a wine glass (not during a tasting) is the "five-ounce pour," which yields five glasses of wine per bottle. When not at a seated dinner, plan on a half bottle of wine for each guest every two hours.

The Oscars

Signature Drink Sign 70

Oscar Ballot 73

Celebrity Swag Bag 70

Trivia Fan 74

Shadow Box Invitation 71

Treat Cone 76

OTHER THAN THE SUPER BOWL, THE ACADEMY AWARDS HAS BECOME *THE* WINTER television event. So roll out the red carpet and create a sophisticated black-tie celeb-worthy soiree, making your home the place to be on Oscar night.

Announce your star-studded gala with shimmering gold-dust paper and crisp black graphics. Begin the evening early so you can watch the red carpet coverage and gossip about designer outfits and celebrity couples as they are interviewed live. Go all out and hire a limo to transport all of your guests. Then enlist a professional "paparazzi" photographer or designate a friend to take snapshots of guests as they arrive.

The Atmosphere

- Purchase, rent, or make a red carpet from fabric or carpet remnants and roll it out from the curb to your door. Absolutely everything else should be black and gold.
- Vintage film reels (available on eBay.com) and unwound rolls of film are the perfect props for tables and counters.
- Add some humor to your event and decorate your bathroom as though it were a dressing room or makeup trailer with props such as boas, sunglasses, fake mustaches, makeup samplers, tiaras, and wigs.
- Purchase classic movie posters and hang them on the walls. Better yet, laminate them and use them to line serving trays. Collage them under a glass-top coffee table or console.
- Print movie quotes on cocktail napkins or coasters.
- Use velvet ropes to section off seating areas, food stations, and televisions.
- Don't forget to dim the lights during the show, bringing them back up for commercial "intermissions."
- Set the mood by playing soundtracks from your favorite Oscar-winning movies before the show begins and even in the background after the show starts.
- Set up televisions in other rooms, some televising the Academy Awards, others playing classic or nominated movies.

- Decorate walls with famous movie quotes, or recreate the Hollywood Walk of Fame stars on your floor in custom removable graffiti appliqués, personalized with guests' names (wonderful graffiti.com).

- Consider hiring a valet service to open car doors as guests arrive on the red carpet.

- Serve a selection of wines from the Rubicon Estate (formerly Niebaum-Coppola Estate Winery), owned and operated for more than 2 decades by legendary moviemaker Francis Ford Coppola.

signature drink sign

Serve Oscar-infused cocktails such as "The Godfather," "The Casablanca," and "The Scarlett O'Hara" in glamorous leopard-patterned glasses (for instructions, turn to the New Year's Eve Signature Drink Sign project on page 146. Get some classic signature drink ideas from drinksmixer.com or drinkswap.com.

celebrity swag bag

Treat every guest like a star and send them home with swag bags filled with theater candy, *Entertainment* and *People* magazines, a movie T-shirt, *Zagat Movie Guide*, DVDs of the year's nominated movies, local movie theater passes, mini Oscar statuettes, and more.

Shadow Box Invitation

(Makes 1 Invitation)

Create a perfect stage for your Academy Awards invitation with a black-and-gold shadow box invitation, and your guests will be dreaming of Oscar. The announcement is framed in etched ribbon scrolls, "Walk of Fame" stars, Art Deco stage lights, a vintage movie camera, admissions tickets, and Oscar himself. Infused with Old Hollywood glamour, this magnificent design is the epitome of celebrity style and indulgence.

MATERIALS
- 3 sheets 8½" x 11" (21.5cm x 28cm) gold card stock
- 2 sheets 8½" x 11" (21.5cm x 28cm) gold text-weight paper
- 1 sheet 8½" x 11" (21.5cm x 28cm) white card stock
- One 2" (5cm) deep 8" (20.5cm) square black box
- Double-sided tape
- One 12" (30.5cm) square cork board tile (sold in packs of 4)
- 4 clear 2" (5cm) wafer seals

TOOLS
- Craft scissors
- Craft knife, self-healing cutting mat, and ruler
- Hot-glue gun

ARTWORK
- Ribbon banners, stars, art deco border, burst clipart, and camera clipart; Oscar statue drawn freehand

INSTRUCTIONS

1 Create a 5-page 8½" x 11" (21.5cm x 28cm) document in your computer page layout or word-processing program.

- Page 1: Place your ribbon banner artwork for your invitation card and set your type on page 1. The frame should be approximately 4" (10cm) high x 6" (15cm) wide. Then place your illustrations of Oscar and 4 stars in varying sizes.
- Page 2: Place a burst no larger than 7½" (19cm).
- Page 3: Place your 8" (20.5cm) art deco frame.
- Page 4: Place crop marks for a 7½" (20.5cm) square mailing label. Typeset your return address in the top left corner.
- Page 5: Place your illustrations of a movie camera and 2 small movie tickets with the host's name and event info. Place a black background behind your tickets and reverse the text to white.

2 Print pages 1 and 2 of your document on gold card stock. Print pages 3 and 4 on gold text-weight paper. Print page 5 on white card stock. Trim around the outside of each piece of artwork printed on card stock, as well as the art deco frame on text-weight paper, leaving about a ⅛" (3mm) border around each piece. Trim your address label to the crop marks.

3 Trim the remaining sheet of gold card stock to fit inside your black box (approximately 7⅞" [20cm] square) and use double-sided tape to attach the card to the base of the box.

4 Cut pieces of the square cork board to stack up behind each piece of cut-out artwork to give

them dimension. Most of the art will only need small pieces of cork, but because you will glue the other art to the burst, it needs more support. For the burst, cut a cork platform only ¼" (6mm) smaller than the art itself. Mount the pieces of cork behind each illustration with a hot-glue gun.

5 To layer your invitation, begin by gluing the burst artwork to the base of the box. After the burst is attached, each layer will be glued to the burst. If you wish to make some stars or other artwork higher than others, add a second or more layers of cork behind them.

6 When the diorama is finished, center your art deco frame on the top of the box opening and fold the outer edges over the side, attaching them to the side of the box with a bead of

hot glue. You'll need to cut a slit in each corner of the frame so the sides lie flat when folded over the box's edge.

7 Put the cover on your box and seal with a clear wafer seal on all 4 sides.

8 Address the label to your guest and turn the label over to apply double-sided tape along all 4 edges, then left-align the label on your box cover, and press it down to adhere, leaving room on the right for postage.

tip

✦ Use the 2003 American Film-making postage or the Hollywood Legends stamps of
Audrey Hepburn, Judy Garland, James Cagney, Cary Grant, or Jimmy Stewart.

Oscar Ballot

(Makes 1 Ballot)

Hand out golden accordion-fold Oscar ballots as guests arrive. Ask them to cast their votes for the winners. Tally scores at the end of the night and award prizes for ballots with the most and least correct choices. (Download the complete nomination list at Oscars.com.)

MATERIALS
- 1 sheet 8½" x 11" (21.5cm x 28cm) gold card stock
- Decorative pen

TOOLS
- Bone folder

ARTWORK
- Ribbon banners clipart

INSTRUCTIONS

1 Create an 8½" x 11" (21.5cm x 28cm) document in your computer page layout or word-processing program. Copy the current Oscar Ballot from Oscar.com or another site and paste it onto your document page. Format the nominees and check boxes, add an "Oscar Ballot" title with the current year and space for guests to write their names and their scores, and embellish with ribbon banner artwork.

2 Print the document on the sheet of gold card stock. Using a bone folder, score and fold the sheet into four even panels.

Trivia Fan

(Makes 1 Fan)

Stylish trivia fans framed by playful banners are personalized with a mix of quotes and facts from the year's nominated movies and your own silver screen favorites. Place them in every room to break the ice and liven up commercial breaks and drawn-out acceptance speeches.

MATERIALS
- 2 sheets 8½" x 11" (21.5cm x 28cm) gold card stock
- ⅛" (3mm) aluminum screw post in antique brass

TOOLS
- Craft scissors
- Craft knife, self-healing cutting mat, and ruler
- ¼" (6mm) hole punch

ARTWORK
- Ribbon banners clipart

INSTRUCTIONS

1 Create a 2-page 8½" x 11" (21.5cm x 28cm) document in your computer page layout or word-processing program. On each page, draw crop marks for 2 trivia cards, each measuring 2½" (6.5cm) wide x 7" high (18cm).

2 Place your ribbon banner artwork on the top right and bottom left of the crop marks, allowing the artwork to bleed past the edges slightly. Set your type for the movie trivia. Repeat on page 2 of your document.

3 Print the document on 2 sheets of gold card stock. Trim your trivia cards to the crop marks, making sure to cut around the outside of the ribbon banner artwork while leaving about a ⅛" (3mm) border.

4 Punch a hole in the same spot in the top-left corner of each card.

5 Collate the cards and bind with your screw post, which can be tightened by hand (no screwdriver needed).

MOVIE TRIVIA

THE SHAWSHANK REDEMPTION

QUESTIONS:

1. What place does Andy ask Red to remember?
2. Name the 2 types of stone Andy wants to carve his chess pieces from.
3. What 3 clues did the police find after Andy's escape?
4. What do the inmates chant when rookie convicts are brought in?
5. What book of the Bible does Andy hide the rock hammer?
6. What 3 movie stars does Andy use to hide his tunnel?

MOVIE TRIVIA

THE PRINCESS BRIDE

QUESTIONS:

1. When Vizzini says, "No more rhyming now, I mean it!" What does Fezzik reply?
2. What was so unusual about Count Tyrone Rugen?
3. What are the 3 terrors of the Fire Swamp?
4. What country does iocane come from?
5. Where is Westley when Prince Humperdinck kills him with The Machine?
6. Who captures Westley when he leaves Buttercup to seek his fortune?

ANSWERS: 1. "Anybody want a peanut?" 2. He had six fingers on his right hand. 3. Flame spurts, lightning sand and R.O.U.S.'s 4. Australia 5. in The Pit of Despair 6. The Dread Pirate Roberts

Treat Cone

(Makes 1 Cone)

Nothing gets you more in the mood for the movies than cinema snacks! Serve them with pizzazz in delicious star-studded treat cones standing in champagne flutes. Fill them with caramel- and butter-flavored popcorn, Milk Duds™, Raisinets™, and Sno-Caps™. The juxtaposition of black-tie attire and concession-stand goodies makes for some great photographic moments.

MATERIALS
- Movie artwork
- 2 sheets 8½" x 11" (21.5cm x 28cm) white text-weight paper
- 1 sheet 8½" x 11" (21.5cm x 28cm) black card stock
- Spray mount
- 1 glass champagne flute
- Movie snacks

TOOLS
- Craft scissors or craft knife, self-healing cutting mat, and ruler

- Glue stick
- Bone folder
- Hot-glue gun

ARTWORK
- Movie art from purchased posters

INSTRUCTIONS

1 Gather, clip out, arrange, and glue (using a glue stick) your movie artwork onto a sheet of white paper. Scan in and print out on the remaining sheet of white paper. The scanned images won't pop off when the printed page is rolled the way they would if they were glued down.

2 In a well-ventilated area, spray adhesive on the reverse side of the printed white paper and attach it to the black card stock. Smooth out any wrinkles using a bone folder.

3 Trim around the edges of the artwork to remove the blank sections of paper (those without collage on them) and make an interesting abstract edge.

4 With the printed side facing out, curl/roll the sheet into a cone shape, overlapping the sides slightly, and use the hot-glue gun to glue it in place with a thin bead of glue at the overlap.

5 Stick the pointed tip into the champagne flute to stand, fill with caramel popcorn or other movie snacks, and serve.

SPECIAL OCCASIONS

Birthday

Pop-Up Invitation 82

Birthday Crown 84

Date Book Favors 87

Birthday Banner 88

Birthday Timeline 88

Surprise-Party Face Masks 90

Circle Menu 92

IF YOU ARE LOOKING FOR AN ALTERNATIVE TO THE TYPICAL CAKE, PUNCH, AND streamers birthday formula, try celebrating like the rich and famous do: Throw an outrageously lavish birthday bash with a pompom theme, complete with pop-up invitation and complementary paperie! If you're celebrating a milestone birthday (and the budget allows), spare no expense and host a weekend of planned events, each with its own theme and location. You probably won't be able to coordinate a military parade or cannon salute fit for royalty, but you can kick off the festivities with a fantastic fireworks display. (Make sure to hire a professional.) Encourage revelry when the guest of honor arrives by providing invitees with confetti and blow horns.

The Atmosphere

Instantly energize the room with vibrant pinks and oranges in fabric, flowers, and ornamentation. If you plan to fill the venue with helium balloons, don't put them in large groups. Instead, opt for a smaller number of 36" (91cm) white, orange, and pink orbs. The bigger the balloon, the more round the shape and the more upscale the look. Or bring a touch of whimsy to your celebration trimmings by using quirky pompom fringe, massive paper pompoms, or paper lanterns in place of streamers.

Use variations in color and pattern on fabric only. Then create arrangements with all types of flowers in the same color scheme.

Monotone florals effortlessly add sophistication to centerpieces.

Hosting Tips

Serve signature drinks in vibrant colors through a fruit infused ice luge to match the décor. Cover a three-layer birthday cake and cake stand with sculpted fondant pompoms or circles. Hire a professional to emcee a toast and roast of the guest of honor. Rent an oxygen bar and choose aromas such as mango, mandarin orange, peach extract, citrus, and watermelon. Hire live musicians to lead everyone in singing an over the top version of "Happy Birthday."

Please arrive no later than 6:30pm, Malissa arrives at 7:00!

Malissa Hunt is turning 31

Join us in celebrating Mal's Birthday on August 16th

The Hunt Home
37 Monatiquot Avenue
in Braintree

Shhhh! It's a Surprise!

R.S.V.P.
to Mira & Ed
at 781.843.4411
by the 1st of August

N°37

Mr. & Mrs.
Stephen Taylor
16 Aldrich Lane
Braintree
Massachusetts
02184

Pop-Up Invitation

(Makes 1 Invitation)

Modern fonts and brilliant shades of pink and orange truly put the *pop* in this pop-up invitation. Using basic folding and assembly techniques, this stunning three-dimensional invitation captures the style of the party décor using a bold combination of circles and stripes. (Shown on page 81.)

MATERIALS

- 3 sheets 8½" x 11" (21.5cm x 28cm) cream card stock
- 1 sheet 8½" x 11" (21.5cm x 28cm) cream crack-and-peel label stock
- 1 A7 (5¼" x 7¼" [13.3cm x 18.5cm]) candy-pink envelope
- Spray mount
- 1 sheet 8½" x 11" (21.5cm x 28cm) candy-pink card stock
- 1 sheet 8½" x 11" (21.5cm x 28cm) or larger decorative text-weight patterned paper
- Double-sided tape
- 3D adhesive foam mounting squares
- 8" (20.5cm) length of decorative pompom trim
- 1½" (3.8cm), 2" (5cm), 2½" (6.5cm), and 3" (7.5cm) hole punches or craft scissors
- Craft scissors
- Craft knife, self-healing cutting mat, and ruler
- Bone folder
- Hot-glue gun
- Pop-up book

TOOLS

- Patterns and folding guide on page 159

ARTWORK

- Computer-drawn circles and stripes

INSTRUCTIONS

1 Create a 3-page 8½" x 11" (21.5cm x 28cm) document. The first 2 pages will be filled with circles for your invitation and will be printed on the cream card stock. The third page will be for the mailing and return addresses for your envelope and will be printed on your label sheet.

- Page 1: Create two 3" (7.5cm) circles. One should announce the guest of honor's name and birthday; the second should give the date, location, and additional details. Create one 2½" (6.5cm) circle and typeset "Shhhh! It's a surprise!" Create two 2" (5cm) circles for the RSVP and arrival information, such as "Please arrive promptly at 6:30 p.m.; the guest of honor arrives at 7 p.m." Color the background of the circles hot pink and orange. Set white invitation type inside each.

- Page 2: Create multiple circles in different sizes ranging from about 2" to 3" (5cm-7.5cm), filling each circle with alternating stripes and circles in different colors using the Birthday Pop-Up Invitation Patterns on page 159. These will be your background circles to add depth and color.

- Page 3: Create 3 circles. The first 2 circles should be 1½" (3.8cm). Typeset one with your return address, the other with a contrasting stripe pattern. The third circle should be 3" (7.5cm), typeset with the mailing address and name of your guest.

2 Print pages 1 and 2 on cream card stock and use your hole punches to punch out each circle. Sharp scissors also work. Print page 3 on crack-and-peel stock and cut them out. Remove the

backing and press them onto the front of your mailing envelope. In the top left corner, layer the return address over part of the striped circle, and place the mailing address circle in the center of the envelope.

3 In a well-ventilated area, spray adhesive onto the back of the candy-pink card stock and adhere it to the back of the decorative paper. Cut the card stock with decorative paper attached to 10" (25.5cm) high x 7" (18cm) wide. Make a score mark at 5" (12.5cm) to fold the card in half for a folded size of 5" (12.5cm) high x 7" (18cm) wide. The candy-pink card should be on the inside and the decorative paper on the outside.

4 To create layered circles inside the invitation card, start with the background layer of decorative circles. Scatter dot- and stripe-filled circles from page 2 of your document around on the card in a visually pleasing way. Attach to the card with double-sided tape. Next attach a second layer of circles with the foam mounting squares, using the instructions in the package. Finally, attach your three-dimensional circles that sit out the farthest from the invitation employing a strip of card stock (use some of the leftovers trimmed from the pink or cream card stock) that is ½" (13mm) wide by 1½" (3.8cm) long.

5 Score and fold the strip of card stock into 3 equal ½" x ½" (13mm x 13mm) sections. (See corresponding folding guide on page 159.) Fold the ends of the card stock strip up to make the shape of a U. Then, make a score mark on the circle card you're attaching that is ¼" (6mm) from the bottom edge and then fold it. Use double-sided tape to attach the back side of the ¼" (6mm) section of the circle card to the bottom panel of your invitation card, ½" (13mm) from the fold of the invitation card. Use double-sided tape to attach the first ½" (13mm) section of the U to the circle and the third ½" (13mm) section of the U to the top part of the invitation card, positioning the lowest end of the U ½" (13mm) up from the invitation card fold. (See the folding guide on page 159.)

6 Close your invitation card and embellish the cover with the pompom trim. Cut the ends of the trim flush with the edges of the card.

tip

✦ When sending out a large number of invitations, use an assembly line approach to create your cards. Line up 10 invitation cards and adhere 10 circles to the top center of each. Next, adhere 10 circles to the middle of the top panel and so on. This will ensure consistency and speed with minimal mistakes.

Birthday Crown

(Makes 1 Crown)

Birthday crowns needn't be reserved for a younger crowd. Creating a luxe version for your guest of honor to wear is an unexpected and loving gesture. Treat the honoree like royalty—sit him or her on a "throne" to be crowned before the gift-opening "ceremony." Have the guest of honor don the crown for a single group photo, or grace the birthday place setting or pile of gifts with this treasure and let the recipient decide if and when to wear it.

MATERIALS

- 2 sheets 16" x 20" (40.5cm x 51cm) or larger decorative text-weight patterned paper (use 2 coordinating patterns for the crown and crown points)
- Spray mount
- 1 sheet 11" x 20" (28cm x 51cm) or larger candy-pink card stock
- 1 sheet 8½" x 11" (21.5cm x 28cm) orange card stock
- ½ yd (45.5cm) orange ¼"- (6mm-) wide decorative felt ribbon or felt rickrack
- 1 sheet 8½" x 11" (21.5cm x 28cm) cream card stock
- ¼ yd (23cm) hot pink ¼"- (6mm-) wide decorative felt ribbon or felt rickrack
- 1 sheet 8½" x 11" (21.5cm x 28cm) cream text-weight paper
- 1 sheet 8½" x 11" (21.5cm x 28cm) pink card stock
- 1 yd (91cm) decorative pompom trim/tassel
- 2 yd (1.8m) raspberry ⅛"- (3mm-) wide grosgrain ribbon

TOOLS

- Templates on page 158
- Craft scissors
- Craft knife, self-healing cutting mat, and ruler
- Hot-glue gun
- ⅛" (3mm) hole punch

ARTWORK

- Computer-drawn circles and stripes

INSTRUCTIONS

1 Using a copier, enlarge the crown template on page 158 so that the width of your crown equals 18½" (47cm). Cut out the crown shape with craft scissors and trace it onto the back side of your decorative paper.

2 In a well-ventilated area, spray the back side of the decorative paper crown shape with adhesive and mount it to the large sheet of candy-pink card stock. With craft scissors, cut the candy-pink card stock into the crown shape, using the edge of the decorative paper as a guide, making sure to cut the pink card stock flush with the edge of the decorative paper.

3 Enlarge the crown-point template on page 158 to 7" (18cm) high, and use it to trace 3 points onto the second sheet of contrasting decorative paper. Cut out the shapes.

4 Spray the back of 2 decorative paper crown points with adhesive and mount them to the orange card stock. Cut the orange card stock to the crown-point shape, leaving a 1/8" (3mm) border all the way around. Hot-glue these 2 points to the left and right points on your crown.

5 Apply a bead of hot glue along the left- and right-hand edges of the center crown point, then attach the orange decorative felt rickrack or ribbon to the back of the point. The felt should be 18" long before attaching to allow a little wiggle room for placement. Trim the ends of the felt flush with the bottom of the point. Use your hot-glue gun to attach the remaining crown point to the center point of the crown, overlapping the inner edges of the rickrack or ribbon.

6 Create a 3-page 8½" x 11" (21.5cm x 28cm) document. Enlarge the oval frame template on page 158 to 2¼" (5cm) high and place on page 1 of the document. Change the color to raspberry or orange and type the birthday year over it.

7 Print page 1 on the cream card stock and trim around the frame. Using your hot-glue gun, put a bead of glue around the edge of the entire oval and attach the hot pink felt rickrack to the back of the oval. The felt should be 9" long before attaching to allow wiggle room during placement. Trim the ends of the felt so they touch but don't overlap. Using your hot-glue gun, attach the center of the oval to the center crown point with the top of the oval 1" (2.5cm) down from the top of the center point.

8 Scan and place the front layer of the crown banner template on page 158, enlarged to 8" (20.5cm) wide, on page 2 of your document. Set type to say, "Celebrate [honoree's name]" or "Make a Wish!"

9 Print page 2 on the cream text-weight paper and trim inside the frame of the banner shape with your craft scissors. Make a "Z" fold on each side of the banner where indicated on the crown banner folding guide on page 158.

10 On page 3 of your document, scan and place the banner template background layer of the crown banner template on page 158, enlarged to 7" (18cm) wide.

11 Print page 3 on the pink card stock and trim inside the frame. Glue the 2 ends of the front folded banner to the 2 ends of the flat background banner. Then glue the center of the flat banner ¼" (6mm) below the oval.

12 Use hot glue to attach the pompom fringe trim around the bottom of the crown. Punch two ⅛" (3mm) holes on each end of the crown where indicated by the crown template. Cut the grosgrain ribbon into four 18" (45.5cm) lengths. Thread ribbon through each of the holes and tie the end into a knot to secure it to the crown. The ribbons allow the crown to be adjustable to any head size.

date book favors

Date book favors, wrapped in matching paper and felt rick-rack, paired with hot pink pens allow guests to mark their own calendars with the get-together plans before they make their exit. Display a yearly calendar and encourage invitees to add his or her birthday and another "date" to spend time with the guest of honor in the coming year.

Birthday Banner and Timeline

(Makes 1 Banner)

Celebrate the guest of honor with a personalized pompom-trimmed birthday banner. Drape it above the gift table or birthday cake and create a photo collage underneath, highlighting milestone events in different sizes labeled with corresponding dates and ages. The more fun and unusual the subject matter, the more interesting the display! Attach the photos and cards to the wall using Sticky Tack so they can be easily removed at the conclusion of the celebration.

MATERIALS

- 13 sheets 8½" x 11" (21.5cm x 28cm) cream card stock to spell "Happy Birthday"
- 1 additional sheet 8½" x 11" (21.5cm x 28cm) cream card stock for each letter of your guest of honor's first name
- Double-sided tape
- Minimum of 2 yd (1.8m) raspberry, orange, or candy-pink mini pompom trim
- Thumbtacks, small brad nails, or decorative upholstery tacks

TOOLS

- Templates on page 158
- Craft scissors
- Hot-glue gun

ARTWORK

- Computer-drawn circles and stripes

INSTRUCTIONS

1 Create a multiple-page 8½" x 11" (21.5cm x 28cm) document in your computer page layout or word-processing program. Scan and enlarge the birthday banner templates on page 158 to create a 3¼" wide (8.2cm) x 4¾" (12cm) high triangle filled with raspberry polka dots and a 2¼" (5.5cm) square rotated 45 degrees filled with an orange burst pattern. Set type inside each square frame for each letter of your banner. Reverse the letter to white. Thirteen pages will make up the letters for "Happy Birthday." Conserve document pages and time by only making one page for the A's and printing it twice, or keep things simple and make one page for each letter in each word. Continue by setting the type for the honoree's name.

2 Print all pages of the document on sheets of cream card stock. Trim each triangle and square card just inside the frame.

3 Use double-sided tape to attach the square letter card to the center of the triangle card to create each banner pennant. Be sure that the top point of the letter card touches, but does not hang over, the straight edge of the top of the triangle card.

4 Line up all banner pennants together to spell out your birthday message.

5 Hot-glue the pompom fringe to the top of each pennant across the top of each triangle.

Surprise-Party Face Masks

(Makes 1 Mask)

Don't want to hide in the dark waiting for your guest of honor? Surprise him or her by having all of your guests hold masks printed with the honoree's face. Imagine your friend entering a party greeted by a sea of her own face staring back at her! For a more upscale look, add ribbon streamers, and paint the Popsicle sticks in alternating pink and orange.

MATERIALS

- 1 jumbo craft wood Popsicle stick
- Gloss acrylic paint (orange, raspberry, or candy pink)
- 1 sheet 8½" x 11" (21.5cm x 28cm) white card stock
- 3" x 7" (7.5cm x 18cm) strip of decorative patterned paper
- 1 yd (91cm) each ⅛"- (3mm-) wide raspberry, orange, and candy-pink satin ribbon (2 of each)
- 8" (20.5cm) decorative pompom fringe trim

TOOLS

- 1"- (2.5cm-) wide foam paintbrush
- Craft scissors
- 9/16" (14mm) hole punch with 4½" (11.5cm) extra-long reach
- Hot-glue gun
- Pinking shears

ARTWORK

- High-resolution color photograph of your guest of honor

INSTRUCTIONS

1 Using the foam paintbrush, paint both sides of your jumbo Popsicle stick with gloss acrylic paint and set aside to dry.

2 Create an 8½" x 11" (21.5cm x 28cm) document in your computer page layout or word-processing program. Scan in and place a high-resolution 8" x 10" (20.5cm x 25.5cm) photograph of the honoree on the page.

3 Print the page onto white card stock, and trim all the way around the face with craft scissors. Use your long-reach hole punch to punch eye holes in the center of each eye. This will allow guests to see the reaction of the guest of honor when he or she arrives.

4 Hot glue the top half of the painted Popsicle stick to the back of the cut-out face mask.

5 Create a rickrack edge all the way around your strip of decorative paper using pinking shears.

6 Fold the decorative paper into the shape of a collar around the top of the Popsicle stick so that it crisscrosses in the front, just underneath the chin of the face mask. Use your creativity to determine the exact placement. Glue the ends together with a hot-glue gun.

7 Cut each length of ribbon into two 18"
(45.5cm) lengths. Bundle all 6 ribbons and tie
them with a double knot around the top of the
collar, just under the chin of the mask, to create
12 ribbon streamers. Cut the ribbon streamers
at a 45-degree angle at different lengths.

8 Use your hot-glue gun to affix the decorative
pompom fringe trim under the chin and over
the collar and ribbon knots, with one pompom
centered under the chin. Fold the ends of the
trim around to the back of the mask, cutting
them so they touch but do not overlap.

tips

✦ Choose pictures
with different
facial expressions:
happy, serious,
surprised, mad, or
silly. The funnier the
expression, the more
amusing for those
who wear it.

✦ Pass the masks out
or display them at
the entrance to the

party so each guest
is prepared when
surprise time comes.

✦ If you have a large
number of guests,
forgo the collar and
ribbon streamers
to save time. The
unembellished
masks will be just
as effective.

*to plan and execute a truly
successful surprise party:*

1 Make sure the guest of honor
truly enjoys surprise parties.

2 Include only trustworthy friends
in the planning so there are no
accidental slip-ups that spoil the
surprise.

3 Arrange for friends to make
plans with the honoree for the
evening. They will accompany
him or her to the party. Make
sure that the plans are signifi-
cant so the honoree doesn't can-
cel at the last minute. Or you can
hire a professional transportation company, ask your guest of
honor to meet you somewhere
public, and surprise him or her
with a bus full of friends and
family for a night on the town.

4 Talk to close friends and relatives to help compose the guest
list.

5 Make it very clear on the invitation that it is going to be a *surprise* birthday party.

6 Ask guests to arrive a minimum of 30 minutes before the
guest of honor, and designate
inconspicuous parking spots for
them.

7 Hand out surprise-party masks
to all guests.

8 Ask the designated friend to
give you a call or send you a text
message before arriving with
the honoree at the party so you
can prepare everyone and have
a camera ready to take pictures!

Circle Menu

(Makes 1 Menu)

Serve the birthday feast on the perfect platform. Layers of color—vibrant table linens under colorful Fiesta® ware—add energy and panache to your decor. Likewise, an unexpected menu shape paired with an interesting napkin fold add playful sophistication to each place setting.

MATERIALS
- 1 sheet 8½" x 11" (21.5cm x 28cm) cream card stock

TOOLS
- Craft scissors

ARTWORK
- Computer-drawn frames and dots

INSTRUCTIONS

1 Create an 8½" x 11" (21.5cm x 28cm) document in your computer page layout or word-processing program. Draw a circle on your page that is at least 1" (2.5cm) smaller than the diameter of your plate or charger. If you are planning a clever napkin fold, make the menu at least 2" (5cm) smaller than the dimensions of the plate and approximately ½" (13mm) smaller than the dimensions of your folded napkin. (My circle was 6½" [16.5cm].)

2 Set dotted and striped frames inside the perimeter of your circle menu. Set the type for your menu selections.

3 Print the menu on the cream card stock and trim around the edge of the circle using craft scissors.

tips

✦ If you do not have a steady cutting hand, try printing a thick four-point frame around the outside of your menu in the same color as your napkin. Cut just inside the frame. This will ensure no white space is showing around the edges, and the edge of the menu will blend seamlessly with your napkin color, minimizing an uneven or shaky edge. Or use the Martha Stewart circle cutter to make a perfect 5½" circle every time.

✦ For creative ideas, simple instructions, and illustrated photographs of napkin folding, I suggest reading *100 Classic Napkin Folds* by Rick Beech.

APPETIZER / SALAD

···

Classic Caesar Salad

with Garlic Focaccia Croutons, Shaved Parmesan
Tossed with Sun-dried and Cherry Tomatoes

·OR·

Crab Ravioli

Home-made Raviolis Plated on top of Scallion Etuvée
with Ginger–Shellfish Béchamel

MAIN COURSE

···

Ricotta Tortellini

with Asparagus and Sun dried Tomato-Basil broth

·OR·

Roasted Sirloin of Beef

Garlic Potato Purée, Wild Mushrooms,
Grilled Asparagus and a Cognac Peppercorn Demi

BIRTHDAY CAKE

···

Anniversary

Custom Cocktail Napkins 97

Pocket Scrapbook Invitation 98

Anniversary Herald 100

Lottery Ticket Favor 102

ANNIVERSARIES ARE MORE THAN JUST THE ANNUAL OBSERVATION AND commemoration of the beginning of a marriage. They can be an annual renewal of vows or a celebration of wedded bliss and are always a wonderful commitment to honor. It does not have to be a milestone anniversary to be party-worthy. Every year that a couple stays together through good times and bad, strengthening their love for each other, is a year to celebrate!

In 2008, my parents celebrated their thirty-fifth anniversary. They are so fortunate to have found each other and even more blessed to have had so many wonderful years together. Through the years, they have touched many lives in a positive way. I could not think of a better way to honor them than to surround them with all of those people at a sumptuous champagne brunch at a chic French brasserie. The fitting theme, "Lucky in Love," was carried through all of their paperie. I chose the soft innocence of blush pink to echo the ribbons that had been woven into the bodice of my mother's wedding dress and that colored her choice of wedding party attire. The touches of antique gold add a vintage look befitting the age of the photographs and date of their wedding.

The Atmosphere

Gilded accents will make your paperie suite and table settings shimmer. Gather photos from throughout the couple's marriage, the sheet music for "their song," and a copy of their wedding invitation and certificate of marriage. Display them in gilt frames surrounded by flowers in blush pinks, creams, and butter yellows.

Use some original items from their wedding day for decoration and recreate others. If the wedding dress is well preserved, display it next to the guest sign-in with a garland of the flowers used in the bride's bouquet. Crown the anniversary cake with the topper from their wedding cake. Or serve an exact replica of their wedding cake. You only need the flavor and a clear picture of

A Champagne Brunch
to Toast

Janet & Ed

AS THEY CELEBRATE
35 BLISSFUL YEARS

Sunday, December 7th, 2008
from 11am until 3pm

BRASSERIE JO

120 Huntington Avenue
Boston

RSVP 617.571.4816   FESTIVE ATTIRE

Edwin Hamilton
Is Married In
Massachusetts

In early December wed-
ding at Epworth United
Methodist Church, Worcester,
Mass., Mrs. Janet Kronoff
Hamei, daughter of Mr.
and Mrs. Frank G. Kronoff
of Northboro, Mass., was married to Edwin H. Hamilton,
son of Mr. and Mrs. Tully
Hamilton, 2904 Pheasant

Given in marriage by her
father, the bride was attended
by her sisters, the Misses
Kronoff and Marcia
Kronoff as maid of honor
and bridesmaid, respectively.
Edward Leckner, Corn-
wall, Pa., was best man.
Hamilton of Whitehall

A reception was held at the
in Braxton, Mass.
The newlyweds now reside

Mrs. Hamilton
graduated from Algon-
quin High, Northboro,
and the groom attended
Clark University, Green-
bush. He graduated from Col-

Forever

DEC
'8
1
9
7
#3

I DO

46695

the cake for most skilled bakeries or cake designers to re-create it.

If you are holding your celebration at a private home, play nostalgic songs from the decade in which the couple was married. For an evening gathering, feature a well-rounded selection of music from past to present, choosing songs with lyrics about love and lasting commitment.

Hosting Tips

Offer scrumptious dishes like apple-smoked-bacon omelets; melon, prosciutto and mozzarella on crisp focaccia toasts; seafood crepes; quiche with fresh strawberries and banana; and strawberry pancakes. (For celebrations later in the day, recreate the menu the couple shared on their first date or on their wedding day.)

Seat the anniversary couple at the same table as the best man or maid of honor from their wedding (with respective spouses).

Toasts are a long-standing anniversary tradition. Encourage everyone to prepare a special tribute or to say a few words about their fond memories of the couple and toast with Laurent-Perrier Cuvée Rosé Brut champagne. It has amazing depth and freshness, is blush pink in color, and, as an added bonus, the label design could not be a better match for the color scheme of this suite. My toast to my parents: "Shakespeare said, 'Journeys end in lovers' meeting.' Here's a toast to thirty-five more years of you two staying put! Thank you for setting such a beautiful example of true love and commitment. Your relationship is an inspiration to all of us."

creating the anniversary herald

Going through my parents' photo collection to create *The Anniversary Herald* newspaper on page 100 was so much fun. What a trip down memory lane! I selected moments that chronicled their lives, from birth to their wedding day through the last thirty-five years to the present (including their baby hospital photos, high school portraits, co-ed bridal shower and wedding snapshots, pictures of them with all six children, Christmas gatherings, and more). I spoke to their parents, my siblings, members of their bridal party, and close friends asking for a brief description of their most special memories with my parents.

I then spent time interviewing my parents, never revealing the reason for my questioning. They knew it was for their anniversary, but not for a commemorative newspaper. They both gave their versions of the day they met, how they fell in love, and the months leading up to their wedding. I added some clever customized headlines and special features: what happened in history the day they were married, a romantic weather forecast, a custom crossword puzzle, and a picture timeline.

Reading the special paper afforded each guest the rare opportunity to share in all stages of my parents' lives, from childhood to the present. It was their history in print, a beautiful way to honor them and the day. I also sent copies to guests who were unable to attend so that no one missed out. Everyone raved about the newspaper. My mother carried it around with her for weeks, sharing it with everyone she knew (and anyone she met!). Later, I had the front page professionally framed for them as a gift.

custom cocktail napkins

Serve guests Bellinis and mimosas accompanied by custom-printed cocktail napkins stamped with the couple's logo in antique gold ink. I branded some with my parents' custom logo and served them with a signature cocktail, Love Potion #35 (a delicious blend of Cherry Kool-Aid®, Grey Goose™ vodka, and coconut rum), on gilt gold trays. (See Resources, page 153, for custom rubber-stamp and inkpad vendors.)

Take a group photograph of the couple and all the guests. Later, add it to the last page of their wedding scrapbook. This is also the most opportune time to update the family portrait! Hire a professional photographer to capture everyone effortlessly in high-resolution, archival images.

Commission a videographer to create a visual montage of the couple's life using still photos mixed with candid interviews and quotes from friends and loved ones. You will be amazed at the great things you learn about your parents from others' perspectives and experiences. Play the video during the seated meal, and provide copies on DVD to all guests.

You won't need to plan many other activities, since anniversary parties are mostly a time for catching up and reminiscing.

Pocket Scrapbook Invitation

(Makes 1 Invitation)

This charming antiqued design features the couple's wedding day photo and newspaper announcement. A separate pearl-edged invitation card tucks into the lace-trimmed pocket at the bottom of the scrapbook page. The gilded treasure is delivered in an antique gold envelope lined in blush-pink lace paper. (Shown on page 95.)

MATERIALS

- 1 sheet 8½" x 11" (21.5cm x 28cm) cream card stock
- 1 sheet 8½" x 11" (21.5cm x 28cm) cream text-weight paper
- 1 sheet 8½" x 11" (21.5cm x 28cm) blush-pink card stock
- Double-sided tape
- 1 sheet 8½" x 11" (21.5cm x 28cm) gold card stock
- 1 large sheet of blush-pink Ogura lace paper, approximately 20" x 30" (51cm x 76cm)
- 5½" (14cm) gold lace
- Velvet leaf and beaded flower embellishments
- 1 package assorted gold Rococo Frames from Blumchen.com
- 21½" (54.5cm) Dresden edging trim
- Two 4" strips of scrapbooking pearl edging
- One package of scrapbooking 4mm clear crystal embellishments
- 1 A9 (5¾" x 8¾" [14.5cm x 22cm]) gold envelope
- 4" (10cm) blush-pink ¼"- (6mm-) wide double-faced satin ribbon
- Typewriter-key alphabet and number stickers

TOOLS

- Craft scissors
- Craft knife, self-healing cutting mat, and ruler
- Hot-glue gun
- Floral hole punch
- Ballpoint pen
- Glue stick

ARTWORK

- Picture of the anniversary couple; newspaper clipping of their wedding announcement

INSTRUCTIONS

1 Create a 2-page 8½" x 11" (21.5cm x 28cm) document in your computer page layout or word-processing program. On page 1, draw crop marks for an invitation card 4½" (11.5cm) high x 3¼" (8.3cm) wide and typeset your invitation inside the crops. On the same page, draw a second set of crop marks measuring 1" (2.5cm) high x 2¼" (5.5cm) wide and typeset the word "Forever" in a script font inside the crop marks. Typeset the words "I DO" in Smackeroo or another decorative block font and place a picture of the anniversary couple measuring roughly 2½" (6.5cm) wide x 3" (7.5cm) high anywhere in the leftover space on the page.

2 Print the page on cream card stock. Trim the 2 cards to the crop marks and trim the photo to the very edge of the image. Then trim around the shape of the words "I DO," leaving ⅛" (3mm) of white space all the way around the letters.

3 On page 2 of your document, scan and place the wedding announcement newspaper clipping. (When making multiple invitations, you will be able to fit more than one per page.)

4 Print the newspaper clipping on cream text-weight paper and trim to the very edge of the image. Cut the pink card stock into 2 rectangles, one measuring 5" x 8" (12.5cm x 20.5cm) and the other 3" x 5" (7.5cm x 12.5cm).

5 Put double-sided tape along the left, right, and bottom back edges of the 3" x 5" (7.5cm x 12.5cm) rectangle no more than ¹⁄₁₆" (1.5mm) from the edge of the card, then adhere it to the bottom of the 5" x 8" (12.5cm x 20.5cm) card to make a pocket, aligning the 5" (12.5cm) edges flush.

6 Using double-sided tape, attach the blush-pink pocketed card to the gold card stock and use craft scissors to trim all the way around the blush-pink card, leaving a ⅛" (3mm) border.

7 Use double-sided tape to attach the newspaper clipping, "Forever" card, and photo of the couple onto your blush-pink card, tucking the bottom edges into the pocket.

8 Embellish your pocket and "I DO" cards: Use your hot glue, double-sided tape, and creativity to add blush-pink lace paper (save enough for the envelope liner you'll make in step 10), gold lace trim, crystals, flowers, fabric leaves, punched-out flowers, and more to your pocket card.

9 Use your hot-glue gun to adhere Dresden trim to the top and bottom edges of your invitation card. Layer a strip of scrapbooking pearls over the Dresden trim on the top and bottom. Tuck the invitation card into the pocket.

10 Line your envelope. Because lace paper has holes in it, you should not use double-sided tape to line the envelope. Instead, slide the lace-paper liner into the envelope and fold the lace paper down at the envelope fold. Using your glue stick, rub a very thin layer of glue all over the envelope flap from ⅛" (3mm) below the glue strip to the fold on the envelope and then unfold the lace paper, pressing it onto the envelope flap to attach it to the glue. Leave the flap open for 10 minutes to allow the glue to dry before inserting the invitation and sealing the envelope for mailing.

The Anniversary Herald

Janet & Ed
FOREVER

DECEMBER 8, 2008

35 YEARS

LUCKY IN LOVE. JANET & ED CELEBRATE THEIR 35TH

35 years. Forever in Love

By Karen Bartolomei

"The phone bill was outrageous," Janet said. They talked often about waiting two to three years before tying the knot. But in the end, saving money was the excuse Janet and Ed tried as justification for getting married so quickly. The truth is, they were their separate ways, after high school graduation, but, three years later, they reconnected and after only a few months, they knew fate had brought them back together.

The "responsible" thing would be to want a while, and develop their relationship, direction they would... ask Janet was a different weekend in 1973.

When Janet went on Memorial Day weekend in Northborough, had been a...

Ed, on his second bowl of ice cream, chimes in quoting Hugh Grant in *Love Actually*, "She was a saucy minx!"

Janet agrees, "I turned a few heads back then"

The final step in her perfect plan: Janet called Ed to ask what he was doing for the holiday weekend, and when he said he had no plans, she invited herself down.

Ed and his father picked Janet up at the airport, and that was the beautiful beginning of the rest of their lives together.

As the months unfolded, they spent hours on the phone each night, they flew back and forth between Pennsylvania and Massachusetts to spend weekends together, and the bills began to pile up. They tried to be moderate with their time together, on the phone and in person, but Love had other plans for them!

They set the wedding date for December 8th and with such a short time to plan, the couple got to work immediately to coordinate all the wedding details.

In the mean time, Janet and her two sisters, Diane and Marcia, had also begun plans for the 25th Surprise Anniversary for their parents, Claire and Frank Kronoff, in September. All the while, Janet and Ed kept flying back and forth between Pennsylvania and Massachusetts to see each other and continue with their wedding plans.

The girls got all the relatives together on both sides of the family – Doanes and Kronoffs – and collected money to send their parents to Bermuda.

They invited their mother and father to Janet's... ment at Upland Gardens in Worcester. Auntie... the grandparents were there. They... with plane tickets and hotel... had never been on a pl... thrilled they had n... in Northborough... looks on the... by forty g...

With... them... kicked... Unit... qua... re...

INSIDE:

Interviews
Family, Friends, and Co-Workers reminisce about their favorite memories with the couple.

January 6th and March 10th
Janet and Ed...on the days they were born. How it all began.

Past, Present and Future
Janet, and Ed have reached three years as...

The Hamilton Family Tree

With the addition of 9 grandchildren from three of their kids, Janet and Ed watch their family tree grow to new heights!

At Home in Templeton

They've had 3 "dream homes" from a turn of the century Colonial to building from the ground up, their current home, practical yet cozy, is their newest dream come true, complete with tranquil outdoor space for their three Treeing Tennessee Brindles.

FORECAST:

Fires of Love cause temperatures to rise on Cloud 9.

INDEX:

Interviews	A
January 6 and March 10	B
Past, Present and Future	B
A Second Honeymoon	C
The Hamilton Family Tree	D
At Home in Templeton	D
Penny, Tully and Lulu	E
10 Day Forecast	E
Pictorial Timeline	E
Crossword Puzzle	

JANET AND ED ON THEIR WEDDING DAY, DECEMBER 8TH, 1973

Sparks Fly at Algonquin High

Peaks and Valleys, Highs and Lows. No Regrets. The Couple Re... Story

...tolomei

...Hamilton was the "...kid in ...med their division...ly. He moved hi...et in C C...

...rying...y call hi...roughout a...ouble hints about...

...ogether and became clo...orcester and, as with al...ough she her feelin...gh he secretly wanted t...

...h school sweetheart" an...ver became serious with...ompared them to a friend told...rs later when a SPARKS, pag...

JANET AND ED CELEBRATE THEIR 35TH

Anniversary Herald

(Makes 1 Herald)

Herald the couple's anniversary date with a commemorative newspaper complete with photographs, stories, a family tree, and a personalized crossword puzzle. Place a newspaper at each place setting, put them in a newspaper rack so guests can pick one up as they arrive, or send them to your guests for delivery on the morning of the couple's anniversary.

MATERIALS
- 1 sheet 11" x 17" (28cm x 43cm) white text-weight paper per newspaper page. Or use legal-size (8½" x 14" [21.5cm x 35.5cm]) or letter-size (8½" x 11" [21.5cm x 28cm]) paper and typeset your newspaper columns accordingly.

ARTWORK
- Photographs of the anniversary couple on their wedding day; current photos of the couple and their family and friends

INSTRUCTIONS

1 Create a tabloid-sized (11" x 17" [28cm x 43cm]) document in your computer page-layout or word-processing program. Use as many pages as you'd like.

2 Set your type and photographs for *The Anniversary Herald*. Include wedding day and current photos of the couple and their family and friends. On the front page, be sure to have a section for the "weather forecast," index, and what's inside the paper. Place a poem on love or marriage at the top of the front page and put clever captions underneath each photo.

3 Print your *Herald* on the front and back of single sheets of 11" x 17" (28cm x 43cm) paper. Collate the flat sheets and fold in half horizontally to 8½" x 11" (21.5cm x 28cm), with the headline showing on the front.

tip

◆ Due to the size limitations of home printers, your *Herald* will most likely not include a spine and will be a series of flat pages collated and then folded in half. To create a tabloid newspaper with spine and fold, set your type and photos on 22" x 17" (56cm x 43cm) pages, and take your files on disc to a digital printer to have them print it on sheets that fold in half to 11" x 17" (28cm x 43cm) like a true newspaper.

Lottery Ticket Favor

(Makes 6 Favors)

Bestow a little luck on guests as they depart. Hang a handful of lottery tickets tucked into glassine envelopes from adorable mini wire hangers personalized with "Lucky in Love" faceplates. Display them on an old wooden door or pickled board studded with square-head nails. I attached tags to my parents' favors that read, "Love is a game of chance. Janet & Ed hit the jackpot!"

MATERIALS

- 6 glassine envelopes, 3⅝" x 5⅛" (9.2cm x 13cm)
- 6 lottery quick-pick cards and $1 or $2 scratch-off tickets
- 2 sheets 8½" x 11" (21.5cm x 28cm) blush-pink card stock
- 6 mini hangers or clips (mine are the Vintage Hanger Clips Wire 6-piece set from Stampington.com)
- 1 sheet 8½" x 11" (21.5cm x 28cm) cream text-weight paper
- 2 yd (1.8m) blush-pink ¼"- (6mm-) wide double-faced satin ribbon
- 6 vintage square-head nails, hooks, or upholstery tacks (My square-head nails came from old hardwood floor remnants in my basement.)
- Old wooden door, shutter, fence post, or board (white or natural wood—the size will depend on how much space you need for the number of favors you are creating. I applied white pickling stain to a 12" x 30" [30.5cm x 76cm] piece of ½"- [13mm-] thick pine board from Home Depot)

TOOLS

- Craft knife, self-healing cutting mat, and ruler

INSTRUCTIONS

1 Cut the flaps off the top of each of your 6 glassine envelopes and slide your lottery cards and scratch tickets inside.

2 Create a 2-page 8½" x 11" (21.5cm x 28cm) document in your computer page layout or word-processing program. On page 1, draw crop marks for a favor tag card 4" (10cm) wide x 3" (7.5cm) high and typeset your message inside the crop marks. Copy and paste this favor tag 3 times on the page.

3 Print the page twice, once on each sheet of blush-pink card stock. Trim the cards to the crops marks.

4 Set one tag on each lottery-filled glassine envelope and clip both to your mini hangers.

5 On page 2, draw crop marks measuring ½" (13mm) high x 1¼" (3cm) wide and typeset the words "Lucky in Love" inside the crop marks. Copy and paste this tag 6 times on the page.

6 Print page 2 on cream text-weight paper. Trim the tags to the crop marks.

7 Slide the tiny tags into the small faceplate on the front of your hangers.

8 Cut the blush-pink satin ribbon into six 12" (30.5cm) lengths. Embellish the neck of each hanger with a pink ribbon bow and hang from nails, hooks, or upholstery tacks on a wooden board or empty wall.

Wedding

Custom Gift Tags. 106

Thank-You Notes. 107

Pocket Invitation. 108

Save the Date 111

Table Number Menu 113

Pocket-Sized Program Book 115

Escort Board and Cards. 116

Postcard Guest Sign-In 118

UNLIKE SOME ASPECTS OF WEDDING PLANNING, THE PAPERIE CAN BE DONE FAR IN advance. With proper strategizing and lots of help from family and friends, you can create a stunning suite of designs—from save the dates and invitations to reception accessories and thank-you notes—that will accent every part of your marriage celebration.

With all the details involved in planning a wedding, it's easy to lose sight of what the day is really about. If you choose to craft your wedding paperie instead of hiring a professional, don't leave everything until the last minute; it always takes longer than you think. Remember, the magic of your wedding day is wrapped up not in the big plans but in the little moments shared with your spouse, your family, and your friends.

The inspiration for this suite came from the groom's proposal at the top of the Empire State Building on Valentine's Day. What better way to reflect the couple's love story than vintage hearts, cupids, and cherubs? The color scheme was chosen from traditional Valentine's Day, forget-me-not, and cupid postcards from the early 1900s. Exuberant shades of snow cone and aqua blue are paired with deep valentine red to convey romance and hint at sensuality. Incorporating clean blocks of color, poems on love, and beautiful hand-scripted calligraphy plays up the mood and adds subtlety to the valentine visuals. This theme does not have to center around Valentine's Day. "Sweetheart" or "love story" motifs work anytime.

Classic color combinations never go out of style. I suggest picking a timeless color combination—fashionable in the 1800s, today, and years from now—or reinterpret a traditional color scheme. You will be looking at the pictures for years to come, so following current fads is not always a good idea.

The Atmosphere

On your wedding day, it is best to leave the decorating in the hands of trusted professionals so that you can concentrate on enjoying yourself. However, the key to this theme is color saturation (blue and red tones) and rich, romantic embellishments, such as tassels, silk runners, curtains, and pillows. Discuss carrying your theme across all elements when you meet with your planner, florist, caterer, cake designer, and linen company.

Some suggestions to start you in the right direction:

- Hang heart-shaped wreaths from the ceremony entrance doors. Blanket the ceremony aisle with red rose petals.

- For an unexpected entrance, select a modern song for the bridal processional and hire classical musicians to play it.

- Use soft rose-colored lighting and gels to cast a dreamy glow over everything.

- Dress your tables in luminous, vibrant blue-silk linens with a red reverse pleat at each corner. Work with your florist to carry the theme throughout. Look to your postcard art for other ideas, including vintage-painted ribbons, crowns, and milagros.

- Mix seating arrangements—square, long, rectangular, circular, and bar-height tables for four—for a welcome visual break.

- Rent red couches and chairs and group them around your dance floor. Add throw pillows for an intimate lounge feel.

- Use a gobo to project your custom monogram in red on an all-white dance floor.

- Have your cake designer recreate your monogram, love poem, or calligraphic flourishes in the cake icing. Serve cookies in the shape of flaming heart *milagros* with your coffee and tea service after dinner.

- Designate someone to adorn the getaway car with a sign incorporating your logo and red-and-blue ribbon streamers. For a dramatic send-off, pass out sparklers to guests and hire live musicians to serenade your getaway.

- Throwing rice at newlyweds is a beautiful tradition that allows your guests to be a part of the celebration and creates some amazing photo opportunities for your wedding album. Stuff your cones with environmentally friendly, biodegradable fillers such as Ecofetti, dried lavender, designer wedding rice, or even real rose petals. Place one cone on the two chairs closest to the aisle on each seating row at the ceremony. If you think guests won't know what to do, print a small tag that says "Toss to a Rosy Future" or "Shower the newlyweds as they walk down the aisle!" (For instructions, see the Treat Cone on page 76.)

custom gift tags

Adorning each place setting with a wedding favor and custom gift tag adds color to your tables, ensures that each guest gets their gift, and eliminates the hassle of an additional favor table display. See page 21 for instructions on how to create custom gift tags.

thank-you notes

Thank-you notes are the grand finale, the last piece of stationery your guests receive from your wedding, so personalize them with your logo and color scheme and write them by hand. I always suggest a flat card. A larger card only exaggerates the shortness of the note, whereas a flat card looks filled with gratitude in only a few sentences. (For instructions, see the Note Cards on page 25.)

Visit your local library or bookstore for help with wording and etiquette for your thank you notes. Here is a simple three-sentence rule to get you started:

1 Thank you for coming to the wedding or sharing in our celebration.

2 Thank you for the gift; name the gift and a personal way you plan to use it.

3 Suggest getting together with the person again soon.

Don't forget to send thank you notes to your wedding party, your officiant, your vendors, and your parents. (For more hosting tips, see The Art of Being a Gracious Host on page 11.)

Hosting Tips

- Create a wedding website to impart travel and wedding details, gift registry, and more. Print the web address on your invitation's travel or direction cards. (My favorite: Wedding Window.com)
- Put together hotel welcome baskets for out-of-town guests. Include local snacks, maps and souvenirs, custom "Do Not Disturb" door hangers with your monogram, local coffee shop gift cards, and a note from you and your fiancé.
- To make your wedding a weekend event, consider a welcome party for all guests in lieu of the traditional rehearsal dinner. Let friends and family reminisce with

you about the best moments of the wedding night at a morning-after brunch.

- Serve guests rosé champagne or rose petal and champagne sorbet as they are being seated at the ceremony, especially on hot summer days.
- Serve drinks, hors d'oeuvres, or bite-sized passed desserts on trays with monogram-printed liners. Stock the bar with cocktail napkins personalized with love quotes, alternating white ink on red napkins and red ink on white napkins.
- Treat guests to a red and blue candy buffet with monogram-printed treat bags.

Pocket Invitation

(Makes 1 Invitation)

One of the most important pieces of mail you will send in your lifetime, contemporary wedding invitations incorporate the traditional and the unconventional when it comes to wording color, presentation, printing techniques, and materials. They are a way to express your personality, as well as the theme, formality, mood, and details of your wedding celebration. This luxurious red-and-blue invitation (also shown on page 105) is modern yet classic, bold yet romantic. The bi-fold pocket design keeps the romantic hand-scripted invitation card at center stage, while staggered cards in the left and right pockets keep all the necessary wedding weekend details in order. With a custom monogram and graceful calligraphy, it makes an unforgettable impression.

MATERIALS

- 5 sheets of 8½" x 11" (21.5cm x 28cm) white card stock
- 1 sheet 8½" x 11" (21.5cm x 28cm) sheer vellum text-weight paper
- Large sheet of card stock for the pocket folder in a vibrant color. Handmade paper comes in odd sizes, so make sure your sheet is big enough to trim down to 13" x 18" (33cm x 45.5cm).
- 5¾" (14.5cm) square white RSVP envelope
- 6½" (16.5cm) square red outer envelope
- Double-sided tape
- 1 sheet of 8½" x 11" (21.5cm x 28cm) blue card stock
- 1 sheet 8½" x 11" (21.5cm x 28cm) white text-weight paper
- 2 yd (1.8m) ¼"- (6mm-) wide hand-dyed silk ribbon

TOOLS

- Template on page 157
- Craft scissors
- Craft knife, self-healing cutting mat, and ruler
- Bone folder

INSTRUCTIONS

1 Create a 7-page 8½" x 11" (21.5cm x 28cm) document in your computer page layout or word-processing program and set up crop marks for the following dimensions (place each card or invitation element on its own page):

Center Panel:

- Invitation card: 5½" (14cm) square
- Border card (a card that is ⅛" larger than the invitation on all four sides creating a visual "frame" around the Invitation): 5¾" (14.5cm) square
- Sheer vellum love quote overlay: 5½" (14cm) square

Left Pocket:

- RSVP card: 5½" (14cm) square

- Reception or brunch card: 5" (12.5cm) wide x 5½" (14cm) high

Right Pocket:

- Travel and accommodations card: 5½" (14cm) square
- Directions or events card: 5" (12.5cm) wide x 5½" (14cm) high

2 Set the type for your invitation card, referring to Wording Etiquette (page 150).

3 Set the type or custom calligraphy for the sheer vellum love quote overlay.

4 Set the type for your 4 staggered enclosure cards, again referring to Wording Etiquette (page 150). Remember that each heading must

RECOMMENDED ACCOMMODATIONS

Biltmore Hotel & Resort
BiltmoreHotel.com • (305) 445-1926
Sonesta Bayfront Hotel Coconut Grove
Sonesta.com • (305) 529-2828
The Grove Isle Hotel & Spa
GroveIsle.com • (305) 884-7683
Ritz-Carlton Coconut Grove Hotel The
RitzCarlton.com • (305) 644-4680
Wyndham Grand Bay Hotel
Wyndham.com • (305) 858-9600

*Note: When making reservations, be sure to mention
the "Laroche/Bennett Wedding" to ensure our special rate.
Reservations must be made no later than*

Travel Information

FRIDAY, JUNE 5TH
CLAMBAKE & COCKTAILS
The Venetian Pool, Coral Gables
7:00pm until 12:00am
*Transportation will be provided to and from the
Lobby of The Biltmore Hotel, Coral Gables
Shuttles run every half hour from 6:30pm until 1:00am*

SATURDAY, JUNE 6TH
WEDDING CELEBRATION
Ceremony
Coral Gables Congregational Church
7:30pm
Reception
The Biltmore Hotel
Country Club Ballroom
immediately following the ceremony

*Transportation will be provided to and from the ceremony.
Shuttles depart from the Lobby of The Biltmore Hotel,
in Coral Gables promptly at 6:45pm*

SUNDAY, JUNE 7TH
FAREWELL BRUNCH
The Biltmore Hotel, Coral Gables
Granada Ballroom Terrace
*anytime between 10:00am and 2:00pm
Join us for brunch when you roll out of bed!*

Weekend Events

Mr and Mrs Peter German
835 Raymond Drive
Coral Gables, Florida 33158

A CELEBRATION
will immediately follow the ceremony
in the spirit of love, laughter, and happily ever after

Country Club Ballroom
Biltmore Hotel
Coral Gables, Florida

Black Tie

Celebration to follow

Mr and Mrs Arthur Gerard Laroche
Request the honour of your presence
at the marriage of their daughter

Zoe Brigitte
to
Ryan Joseph Bennett

Saturday the sixth of June
Two thousand and nine
at half past seven in the evening
Coral Gables Congregational Church

THE FAVOUR OF A REPLY IS REQUESTED
BEFORE THE TWENTY-THIRD OF MAY

M_____

___ Accepts   ___ Regrets

___ Wedding Celebration Saturday Evening
___ Clambake and Cocktails Friday Evening
___ Farewell Brunch Sunday Morning

___ Aged New York Sirloin
___ Striped Sea Bass Filet
___ Vegetarian

Kindly Respond

Laroche Family
55 Brickell Bay Drive
Apartment 18
Miami, Florida, 33131

Some people
wait a lifetime
for a moment
like this.

It's a shame that the work of a professional calligrapher is often reserved for addressing envelopes. I highly recommend using a calligrapher to create a couture font for your invitation and accessories. It costs a bit more, but it adds extravagance and personalization to your names and wedding information like no other form of artwork. As an added bonus, you can be sure that the calligraphy on your invitation will perfectly match the addresses on your envelopes! If hiring a professional for the entire invitation seems a bit costly or time prohibitive, consider only scripting your names, your monogram, and the headlines of your enclosure cards.

Keep in mind that all calligraphers, like all artists, have a unique style. You must do some research to find a style that matches your personality and the mood of your wedding. For this invitation design, I chose Larry Orlando. A master at his craft, he not only matches his calligraphy and ink colors to invitations printed with computer fonts, but will create custom fonts, monograms, flourishes, and more upon request.

fit completely into the ½" (13mm) from the leading edge (right edge for left-pocket cards; left edge for right-pocket cards) of the card so the card in front does not cover it. Stagger the enclosure cards with reception card in front and the RSVP card and RSVP envelope behind on the left side, and the accommodations, directions, and events cards in that order on the right.

5 Print the invitation and enclosure cards onto the 8½" x 11" (21.5cm x 28cm) white card stock, print the poem or quote onto sheer vellum, and trim all designs to the crop marks.

6 Set the type for the addresses on the outer envelope so that it will print in the top center of the flap. Set the type for the front of your RSVP envelope so it will print in the dead center of the envelope. Print the RSVP address on the front of the 5¾" (14.5cm) square RSVP envelope using the manual feed tray on your printer. Print the return address on the flap of the 6½" (16.5cm) square outer envelope, again using the manual feed tray.

7 Using the Pocket Invitation template on page 157, cut the 13" x 18" (33cm x 46cm) card stock to the dimensions of the template. The "V" in each pocket should be 1¾"(4.5cm). Create score marks where the template indicates folds for each panel and flap for tape. Fold at score marks, using the flat edge of the bone folder to smooth the fold. Then flatten the pocket folder and attach double-sided tape to the 2 flaps on each pocket. Fold the flaps inward and fold the pockets closed, sticking the flaps to the inside of the pockets.

8 Trim the border card from your blue paper using the dimensions in step 1 as a guide. Using double-sided tape, attach your invitation card to the center of the border card, then tape the border card to the center panel of the pocket folder completed in the previous step with double-sided tape along all four of the card's edges.

9 Tuck the RSVP card, RSVP envelope and the reception card into the left pocket and the ac-

commodations, directions, and events cards into the right pocket, and close the pocket invitation folder, with the left flap folded over the right.

10 Tie decorative silk ribbon around the outside of the folded pocket invitation folder. If you wish, crisscross the ribbon.

11 Create another 8½" x 11" (21.5cm x 28cm) document for your envelope liner and place the 2-letter monogram in the top half of the layout. Fill the background with blue and reverse the monogram design to white.

12 Print the envelope liner design on the sheet of white text-weight paper. Set your outer envelope with the flap open on the printed liner paper. Trace around the outside of the envelope, and then trim ¼" (6mm) inside the line.

13 Place double-sided tape on the back of the liner and slide it into envelope. Press down to adhere. Insert the pocket invitation folder into the outer envelope with the front facing the flap.

tips

✦ If you need to add more information to your invitation, such as weekend events, rehearsal dinner information, or directions and a custom map, print it on the backs of the cards.

✦ Whether contained in the welcome baskets, handed out at the ceremony site or inserted into the invitations, directions should be functional and cheery. Include a keepsake map and driving routes to the ceremony and from the ceremony to the reception.

✦ Another clever way to give directions to your guests and save on paper waste is the website DialDirections. com. When guests call (347) 328-4667 (DIRECTIONS) and say your event name, the site will text them directions. The service is free for you and only costs the caller the price of receiving the text message.

Save the Date

(Makes 1 Save-the-Date Card)

Invite your guests to save the date with a vintage-inspired valentine, complete with a lush pop-out tissue-paper heart in the shape of a *milagro* (Spanish for *miracle*), a devotional charm that symbolizes the spell of love. (Shown on page 112.)

MATERIALS

- 1 sheet 8½" x 11" (21.5cm x 28cm) white card stock
- One 5" (12.5cm) red half-round art-tissue heart decoration
- Spray mount
- 1 sheet 8½" x 11" (21.5cm x 28cm) red text-weight paper
- Double-sided tape
- 1 red A2 (4⅜" x 5¾" [13.3cm x 18.5cm]) envelope

TOOLS

- Craft scissors
- Craft knife, self-healing cutting mat, and ruler
- Bone folder

ARTWORK

- Vintage cupid artwork from postcard art from my own collection

INSTRUCTIONS

1 Create an 8½" x 11" (21.5cm x 28cm) document in your computer page layout or word-processing program and draw frames or crop marks and score marks for your save the date cover. (My cover is 8¾" x 5¾" [26.5cm x 18.5cm], folding to 4⅜" x 5¾" [13.3cm x 18.5cm]) when closed.)

2 Scan and place the vintage postcard art. Set the type for the inside of the cover. I used the anonymous quote, "Once in a while, right in the middle of an ordinary life, Love gives us a fairy tale." Other important information to include: the couple's name, wedding date and location, and "Please save the date, invitation to follow."

3 Print the cover on the sheet of white card stock. In a well-ventilated area, spray adhesive on the blank outside of the printed cover and attach it to the sheet of red paper. This will add visual interest and weight to your save the date by creating a red outer cover. Trim to the crop marks. Use your bone folder to score and fold the card in half.

4 Cut your tissue heart down to fit in the gutter of your folded card. Mine is 3¾" (9.5cm) high x 2½" (6.5cm) wide when open. I cut mine to resemble a heart with a flaming crown.

5 Using double-sided tape, attach your tissue paper heart to the center of your save the date by tucking the folded heart into the center of the folded card and pressing it closed to adhere.

monograms

Monograms are a beautiful and popular ornament for wedding invitations. Keep in mind that a monogram using the married surname initial is considered improper etiquette before the ceremony has taken place. Married monograms are reserved for all paperie afterwards: menus, escort cards, thank-you notes, and favor boxes.

However, it is perfectly acceptable to use first initials to create a two-letter monogram before and after the ceremony. For fully hand-calligraphed, square invitation cards, the traditional placement of the monogram above the text does not work well. Instead, use it unexpectedly to personalize the envelope liner.

Table Number Menu

(Makes 1 Menu)

Mark your tables and feature menu selections for the upcoming feast with gorgeous calligraphed table numbers that double as menus. Ornamental, practical, and functional, they blend with your centerpiece and table linens and cut down on paper waste and assembly time.

MATERIALS
- 1 sheet of 8½" x 11" (21.5cm x 28cm) white card stock
- Double-sided tape
- 1 sheet of 8½" x 11" (21.5cm x 28cm) blue card stock
- One 6" x 8" (15cm x 20.5cm) folding easel or frame

TOOLS
- Craft scissors
- Craft knife, self-healing cutting mat, and ruler

INSTRUCTIONS

1 Create an 8½" x 11" (21.5cm x 28cm) document in your computer page layout or word-processing program and draw crop marks for a single flat card measuring 5" (12.5cm) wide x 7" (18cm) high.

2 Scan your calligraphed table number and place it and your menu text inside the frames.

3 Print the document on a sheet of white card stock. Trim your cards to the crop marks.

4 Using double-sided tape, attach the printed menu to the blue card stock.

5 Trim the blue card stock, leaving an ⅛" (3mm) border on each side.

6 Using double-sided tape, attach the layered menu to the center of one side of the fabric-covered easel.

tips

✦ For your interior pages, consider including a title page with the names of the bride and groom as well as the ceremony date and location, plus the following information in this order:

    Poem or Quote

    Wedding Party

    Order of Ceremony

    Wedding Traditions Explained

    History of the Wedding and reception locations

    Story of how the couple met

    Special Thanks

    In Loving Memory

✦ Instead of typesetting all of your pages, have a custom calligrapher write each section heading and a flourished swirl to separate each section.

✦ At the event, explain the concept on a sign above the revolving postcard rack. Set your programs on each seat or have your ushers hand them out to each guest as they arrive at the ceremony location.

Pocket-Sized Program Book

(Makes 1 Program)

A mini booklet, small enough to fit inside a woman's clutch or a man's suit coat pocket, is a brilliant presentation that will ensure programs won't be left behind at the conclusion of your ceremony, At my request, Larry Orlando created this beautiful intertwining script monogram of the couple's first initials symbolizing the joining of their lives together. Inside are more scripted poems on love, ceremony details, the wedding party list, and a special thank you to all guests for sharing in the joy of their union. A nontraditional binding of beaded wire, cord, and blue peacock yarn adds softness and texture to the cover.

MATERIALS
- 1 sheet of 8½" x 11" (21.5cm x 28cm) white card stock
- 5 sheets of 8½" x 11" (21.5cm x 28cm) white text-weight paper
- 18" (45.5cm) Sensations Blue Peacock yarn from Joann.com
- 10" (25.5cm) blue 20-gauge beading wire
- 10 blue glass beads in various sizes and shapes

TOOLS
- Craft scissors or craft knife, self-healing cutting mat, and ruler
- ¼" (6mm) hole punch

INSTRUCTIONS

1 Create a 5-page 8½" x 11" (21.5cm x 28cm) document in your computer page layout or word-processing program and draw crop marks for a program cover and pages that measure 3¾" (9.5cm) wide x 5½" (14cm) high. (You will be able to fit 2 program pages on each of your document pages.) The front cover and back cover should be laid out on the same page. Place a solid blue background on the front and back covers, allowing the background to bleed off the edges. Place your monogram artwork on the front cover inside the crop marks and reverse the color of the monogram to white.

2 Set the type and artwork for your interior pages, leaving ¾" to 1" (2-2.5cm) at the top of the program for your holes.

3 Print the cover on white card stock and the interior pages on text-weight paper. Trim each page to the crop marks.

4 Punch 5 holes across the top of each page with a hole punch. (You will be able to punch both back and front covers together, and up to 5 text-weight pages together.)

5 Collate the cover and pages and bind by threading the peacock yarn through the holes in a random pattern. Leave a tail at each end of the yarn measuring approximately 2" (5cm).

6 Thread the blue beading wire through the holes, adding beads at random intervals as you go and curling the ends to secure the final beads onto the wire.

Escort Board and Cards

(Makes 1 Board with 20 Cards)

Your escort or seating card display presents another wonderful opportunity to personalize your celebration where guests naturally congregate. Typically table cards are stuffed into envelopes personalized with guests' names, or tented cards are calligraphed with names and table assignments on the front. Take a cue from your invitation design and give colorful hand-scripted cards a dramatic backdrop. Help guests find their seats using a decorative paper-covered magnet board. Organize your escort cards alphabetically by last name in neat rows with red silk dupioni button magnets.

MATERIALS

- 1 large sheet decorative paper with a minimum size of 14" x 26" (35.5cm x 66cm)
- Double-sided tape
- 1 metal dry-erase or magnet board (approximate dimensions: 12" x 24" [30.5cm x 61cm])

- 4 sheets 8½" x 11" (21.5cm x 28cm) blue card stock
- 20 fabric-covered flat-back button kits, size 24 (⅝" [16mm] diameter)
- ⅛ yd (11cm) red silk dupioni fabric
- 20 circular self-adhesive craft magnets, ½" (13mm) diameter

- 1 yd (91cm) 2" (5cm) wide decorative ribbon (optional for hanging purposes)

TOOLS

- Craft scissors
- Craft knife, self-healing cutting mat, and ruler

INSTRUCTIONS

1 Measure the total width and height of the front and side edges of your magnet board and trim the decorative paper to that size.

2 Attach double-sided tape all the way around the 4 edges or sides of the magnet board. Set your decorative paper face down on a clean surface. Set your magnet board face down onto the center of the paper and wrap the left- and right-hand sides of the paper around the board's side edge. Fold the corners in on a diagonal as you would a gift-wrapped box, and wrap the top and bottom edges around the board's side edge.

3 Trim each sheet of your blue card stock to make six 2¾" x 2¼" (7cm x 5.5cm) cards. Have a professional calligrapher inscribe names and table numbers onto each card in white ink.

4 Set the button top from the kit on your silk fabric and cut twenty ⅞" (2.2cm) circular pieces from the silk (or circles ¼" [6mm] larger than your button kit size). Wrap the edges of one fabric circle around the metal teeth on the edge of the button top. Snap the flat back into place on the back of the button to secure the fabric. Repeat for the remaining buttons.

5 Peel off the protective backing and attach a craft magnet to the flat back of each fabric-covered button.

6 Hang your magnet board from wide decorative ribbon or prop up with a table-top easel and arrange cards in alphabetical order on the board, hanging each card with a magnetic fabric-covered button.

tips

✦ For larger guest lists, hang multiple boards vertically from thick satin ribbon, or line them up side by side on floor or table easels.

✦ Set up the display near the entrance to the reception so that guests can pick up their seating assignments during cocktails or as they are ushered to dinner tables.

Postcard Guest Sign-In

(Makes 10 postcards, 1 Instruction Sign, and 1 Optional Monogram Faceplate)

I created one of my all-time favorite guest sign-in concepts, the vintage postbox display, for my own wedding in 2002. The response from my guests was so overwhelming, I just have to share it! Guests are asked to write their good wishes to the bride and groom on postcards and then "mail" them in the postbox. A volunteer mails the cards after the reception, and, returning from the honeymoon, the happy couple is greeted by a mailbox filled with joyful notes from family and friends.

MATERIALS
- 6 sheets 8½" x 11" (21.5cm x 28cm) white card stock
- Double-sided tape
- Postcard rack
- Postbox or container for signed cards
- Matching decorative pens

TOOLS
- Craft knife, self-healing cutting mat, and ruler

ARTWORK
- Vintage postcards

INSTRUCTIONS

1 Create a 7-page 8½" x 11" (21.5cm x 28cm) document. On 6 of the pages, draw crop marks that measure 3½" (9cm) high x 5½" (14cm) wide. (You will be able to fit 2 postcards on each of your pages.) The first 5 pages will have postcard art for the front of the postcards. Page 6 will be the back side for all postcards, so make sure the crop marks are centered and in the same place on each page.

2 Place your artwork on each page inside the crop marks. Typeset your 6th page with space on the left for the guests' messages and space on the right for the couple's home address.

3 Print the first 5 pages on white card stock. Turn the pages over and print page 6 (the back of the postcard) on the back of each of the first 5 pages. Make sure the crop marks on the back line up with the ones on the front of each postcard. Test the alignment on scrap paper first. (Print enough postcards to have one per single guest or couple.) Trim to the crop marks.

4 On page 7 of your document, draw crop marks and design your instruction sign for your postcard rack and the monogrammed faceplate for your postbox. The size of each will vary depending on your rack and box. Print, and slide the sign into the holder on the postcard rack. Use double-sided tape to adhere the monogrammed faceplate to your postbox.

HOLIDAYS

Holiday Gathering

Songbook Invitation 125

Holiday Recipe Stocking Stuffer 127

Wish tree Sign-In 130

Scrap-Paper and Tinsel Ornament 132

Holiday CD Favor 134

LIVING IN THE NORTHEAST HAS BEEN BOTH A BLESSING AND A CURSE. EVERY year from winter to spring, there's endless cold, snow, slush, wind, and freezing rain, sometimes until May! The upside? Every December comes the perfect winter weather: falling snow, icicles clinking together in the wind like enchanted wind chimes, and early sunsets that show off the holiday lights, which in turn create the perfect backdrop for the stars and glimmering snow in the moonlight.

The wintry weather adds so much sparkle, coziness, warmth, and authenticity to the holidays. I think back to all those mornings my brother, four sisters, and I woke up early to listen for school cancelations, hoping for a snow day. I remember the sting in my nose from breathing in the cold winter air while in the woods at my parents' house. Making perfect snow forts until I couldn't feel my fingers and toes anymore. Decorating cookies while eating the raw dough and sugar sprinkles. Making paper and felt ornaments while waiting impatiently for my parents to hang all the lights so I could begin trimming the tree.

Capture all of these wonderful winter memories in your holiday paperie suite—an invitation, guest sign-in, stocking stuffer, ornament, and party favor. If you recreate this magical feeling for your guests, they will undoubtedly recall their own special childhood memories. You will stir up the perfect spirit of giving and sharing for the season!

To truly capture the spirit of the holidays with your paperie suite, look to the past for inspiration. The delicate vintage ornaments, traditional fabric patterns, charming illustrations, and holiday carols from the eighteenth and early nineteenth centuries can add elegance to today's often hyper-commercialized festivities.

Consider traditional and nontraditional color combinations: red and green, blue and silver, black and white, silver and gold, or even shabby-chic pink and creamy white. Select a color scheme that evokes warmth and holiday cheer, but make sure it coordinates with your home, as your decorations will be up for weeks surrounding the holidays!

From: DIANE & ADAM PORTER
       761 BELLEVUE AVENUE,
       NEWPORT, RHODE ISLAND
       0 2 8 4 0

To: *Mr. and Mrs. John Hamilton*

     515 SOUTH STREET
     TEMPLETON, MASSACHUSETTS
     0 1 4 6 8

SO COME SHARE
THE WARMTH OF THE SEASON
ON DECEMBER 20, 2008

AT

Our 5th Annual

Victorian Tree Trimming Gala

761 BELLEVUE AVENUE, NEWPORT

COCKTAILS & SWEETS
FROM SIX O'CLOCK UNTIL MIDNIGHT

DIANE & ADAM PORTER
(401) 767 5870
JINGLE OUR BELL · REGRETS ONLY

Let it Snow!

The Atmosphere

Turn your home into a fairy tale. Twist evergreen up your banisters. (Cedar works best and sheds the least.) Don't relegate the Christmas tree to your living room—put trees in multiple rooms! Every October, my husband and I drive to a Christmas tree farm and tag five trees, one for each room. We go back again the day after Thanksgiving to claim them, and then we decorate each of them with a different theme or color scheme: red and green candy canes and Shiny Brite® ornaments from the 1950s on one, crocheted snowflakes and beaded garlands on another. I trim the branches with vintage ornaments collected from estate sales, junk shops, antiques fairs, and online auctions over the years. Even the gift wrap and adornments under each tree reflect the room decor.

Purchase an old, wooden, Flexible Flyer® sled from a yard sale or antiques shop and prop it at your front door. Pair it with an arrangement of evergreens and pinecones tied with a festive bow. Affix silver bells to the toes of an old-fashioned pair of leather children's skates and hang them by the laces over the bars of the sled. Dangle authentic sleigh bells from your front doorknob to announce each guest with festive holiday chimes. A secondhand trumpet wrapped in a big satin bow is the perfect touch for the bar.

Songbook Invitation

(Makes 1 Invitation)

New holiday songs come out every year, but the old standards just can't be replaced. For this holiday invitation (also shown on page 123), I used the sheet music from "Let It Snow." A beautiful postcard of a winter scene from 1905 edged in silver vintage Dresden trim graces the cover. The book opens to reveal a sheer vellum sheet printed with a snowflake pattern to soften the transition from cover to inside pages.

MATERIALS
- 1 sheet 8½" x 11" (21.5cm x 28cm) white card stock
- 1 sheet 8½" x 11" (21.5cm x 28cm) sheer vellum text-weight paper
- 2 sheets 8½" x 11" (21.5cm x 28cm) white text-weight paper
- Spray mount
- 1 sheet 8½" x 11" (21.5cm x 28cm) navy text-weight paper
- 21½" (54.5cm) Frilly Fleuron Dresden edging trim
- Three 18" (45.5cm) lengths of white angora yarn
- 1 light blue A7 (5¼" x 7¼" [13.3cm x 18.5cm]) envelope
- Double-sided tape

TOOLS
- Craft scissors
- Craft knife, self-healing cutting mat, and ruler
- Bone folder
- Hot-glue gun

ARTWORK
- Vintage snowflake clipart, vintage postcard art from my collection, and "Let It Snow" sheet music

INSTRUCTIONS

1 Create a 3-page 8½" x 11" (21.5cm x 28cm) document in your computer page layout or word-processing program and draw crop marks and score marks for your invitation cover and pages. (My cover is 10" x 7" [25.5cm x 18cm], folding to 5" x 7" [12.5cm x 18cm]. To ensure they don't stick out beyond the edges of the cover, my inside pages are 9¾" x 7" [24.8cm x 18cm], folding to 4⅞" x 7" [12.4cm x 18cm].) Your document will need two pages for the invitation's interior pages; one will be for the sheet music and event details, and the other will be for the vellum insert.

2 Set the type for the cover and pages. Scan in and place a vintage postcard on the cover, adding the title "Let It Snow!" Scan in the sheet music and snowflake images and place them on the interior pages. Copy and paste multiple snowflakes at various sizes to create an all-over snowstorm pattern on the sheer vellum between the cover and pages.

3 Print the cover on the sheet of white card stock. Print the snowflake pattern on the sheet of sheer vellum. Print the interior pages on one sheet of white text-weight paper.

4 In a well-ventilated area, spray adhesive on the back of the printed cover and attach the cover to the sheet of navy paper. The dark blue inside layer will add visual interest and weight to your cover. Trim your cover and pages to the crop marks. Using your bone folder, score and fold each piece of paper in half crosswise.

5 With your hot-glue gun, attach the Dresden trim around the image on the postcard cover.

6 Gather all 3 strands of angora yarn together and tie a knot at one end. Braid the strands to the end and tie another knot. Collate the cover, vellum, and pages. Wrap the braided yarn along the book's spine from the outside bottom to the top, and then back down the inside of the spine.

Tie the ends together where they meet at the bottom of the spine.

7 Create a document for your A7 envelope addresses that is 7¼" [18.5cm] wide x 5¼" [13.3cm] high. Typeset the addresses with the same fonts from the invitation. Using the manual feed tray on your printer, print the guest address on your envelopes.

8 Create another 8½" x 11" (21.5cm x 28cm) document for your envelope liner and place the sheet music in the layout.

9 Print the envelope liner on the remaining sheet of white text-weight paper and follow instructions for lining your envelope on page 10.

Holiday Recipe Stocking Stuffer

(Makes 2 Recipe Cards and 1 Decorative Wrap)

As a favor or a stocking stuffer, these recipe cards are sure to make mouths water. Recipes for candy-cane cocoa, eggnog cheesecake, peppermint bark, or favorite treats from your childhood will get everyone in the mood to do some holiday baking!

MATERIALS

- 2 sheets 8½" x 11" (21.5cm x 28cm) white card stock
- Double-sided tape
- 1 sheet 8½" x 11" (21.5cm x 28cm) navy card stock
- 1 sheet 8½" x 11" (21.5cm x 28cm) pale blue textured card stock
- 21½" (54.5cm) Frilly Fleuron Dresden edging trim (sold in packages of 10 strips)
- Spray mount

TOOLS

- Craft scissors
- Craft knife, self-healing cutting mat, and ruler
- Hot-glue gun
- Bone folder

ARTWORK

- Vintage frame clipart; vintage postcard art from my own collection

INSTRUCTIONS

1 Create a 2-page 8½" x 11" (21.5cm x 28cm) document in your computer page layout or word-processing program and draw crop marks on each page (in the exact same location) for two recipe cards that each measure 5" (12.5cm) wide x 3" (7.5cm) high. You will use page 1 to lay out the decorative frame and title of the recipe and page 2 to typeset the ingredients and preparation. Scan and place the decorative frame artwork on page 1 inside the crop marks for each card. Typeset the name of the recipe inside each frame. Typeset ingredients and preparation instructions inside the crop marks on page 2 of your document.

2 Print page 1 of the document on a sheet of white card stock. Flip the card over and print page 2 of the document on the back side. Trim your cards to the crop marks.

3 Create another 8½" x 11" (21.5cm x 28cm) document in your computer page layout or word-processing program for your "Holiday Recipes" tag and draw crop marks that measure 3" (7.5cm) wide x 2" (5cm) high. (If you are creating stocking stuffers for more than one person, you can fit 4 of these tags on one page.) Scan and place the decorative frame artwork on page one inside the crop marks for each card. Typeset the title "Holiday Recipes" inside the frame.

4 Print the document on the remaining sheet of white card stock. Trim your card to the crop marks.

5 Use double-sided tape to adhere the tag to the sheet of navy card stock and trim around the tag, leaving a ⅛" (3mm) border all the way around the card.

Holiday Recipes
2008

From the Kitchen of Diane Porter

INGREDIENTS:
3 (1 ounce) squares semisweet chocolate, chopped
4 cups milk
4 peppermint candy canes, crushed
1 cup whipped cream
4 small peppermint candy canes

DIRECTIONS:
In a saucepan
peppermint ca
whipped cream

Candy Cane Cocoa

Candy Cane Cocoa

6 Trim the pale blue decorative card stock to 3½" (9cm) wide x 7" (18cm) high. Use double-sided tape to adhere the layered tag to the center of the pale blue decorative textured card stock.

7 Cut two 7" (18cm) lengths of Dresden edging trim and use your hot-glue gun to attach one each to the left- and right-hand sides of the pale blue decorative card stock. Place the bead of glue on the back of the trim and then place it on the card stock.

8 Center the tag on the front of the bundled recipe cards. Use the bone folder to score and fold the ends of the wrap completely around the cards, using double-sided tape to attach the ends together where they meet in the back.

---

tip

✦ If you are having a hard time lining up the back and front of your recipe cards, you can print each separately, trimming the recipe side slightly smaller (1⁄16" or 1⁄8" [1.6–3mm]) than the title and frame side, and adhere the two sides together with double-sided tape or spray adhesive.

candy cane cocoa

4 cups milk

3 (1 ounce) squares semisweet chocolate, chopped

4 peppermint candy canes, crushed

1 cup whipped cream

4 small peppermint candy canes

In a saucepan, heat milk until hot, but not boiling. Whisk in the chocolate and the crushed peppermint candies until melted and smooth. Pour hot cocoa into four mugs, and garnish with whipped cream. Serve each with a candy cane stirring stick. Makes 4 servings.

Wish Tree Sign-In

(Makes 1 Tree Sign, 8 Wish Tags)

Invite your merry arrivals to pen their deepest Christmas wishes on tiny precious cards adorned with miniature silver sleigh bells. Hang them from the branches of the wish tree and all their wishes are sure to come true on Christmas day!

MATERIALS

- 2 sheets 8½" x 11" (21.5cm x 28cm) white card stock
- Spray mount
- 1 sheet 8½" x 11" (21.5cm x 28cm) navy text-weight paper
- Eight 7" (18cm) lengths pale blue or white ⅛"- (3mm-) wide velvet ribbon
- Eight ¼" (6mm) mini silver craft jingle bells
- 1 sheet 8½" x 11" (21.5cm x 28cm) light blue text-weight paper
- 1 sheet 8½" x 11" (21.5cm x 28cm) navy text-weight paper
- Tabletop-sized tree (wire, feather, or live)

TOOLS

- Craft scissors
- Craft knife, self-healing cutting mat, and ruler
- ⅛" (3mm) hole punch
- Bone folder

ARTWORK

- Vintage frame clipart; vintage postcard art from my own collection

INSTRUCTIONS

1 Create an 8½" x 11" (21.5cm x 28cm) document and draw crop marks for 8 wish tags that each measure 2¾" (7cm) wide x 2" (5cm) high. Scan and place the decorative frame artwork inside the crop marks for each card.

2 Print the document on a sheet of white card stock. In a well-ventilated area, spray the adhesive on the back of the printed card stock, and attach it to the sheet of light blue text-weight paper. This light blue backing on each card will add visual interest and weight. Trim your tags to the crop marks.

3 Punch one centered hole about ½" (13mm) from the top and bottom edges of each card.

4 Thread one length of the velvet ribbon through the holes and finish by threading a single silver jingle bell onto the tail of the ribbon. No knotting or gluing is necessary to keep

the bell and tag in place—the thickness of the velvet ribbon threaded through the small holes prevents them from slipping. Repeat this step for the remaining 7 wish tags.

5 Create an 8½" x 11" (21.5cm x 28cm) document and draw crop marks and score marks for a 6" (15cm) wide x 8" (20.5cm) high wish-tree tent sign. The sign will fold in half to a finished size of 6" (15cm) wide x 4" (10cm) high.

6 Scan and place the decorative frame artwork inside the crop marks. Typeset your message inside the decorative frame.

7 Print the document on the remaining sheet of card stock. Spray adhesive on the back and attach it to the sheet of the navy text-weight paper. Score and fold your sign in half crosswise. Set your sign flat again and trim to the crop marks.

Peace on Earth
DEANA GRANT

A new bike!
Bob Allen

The Wish Tree
Hang your Christmas wish from it's branches
and it will come true!

Scrap-Paper and Tinsel Ornament

(Recipe Makes 1 Star and 1 Oval Ornament)

To kick off your tree-trimming gala, ask each guest to pick a traditional Victorian scrap-paper and tinsel ornament and hang it from a white feather tree. Originally produced in Germany in the mid-1800s to save the diminishing evergreen forests, white feather trees are the perfect canvas for your hand-made ornaments.

MATERIALS

- Scrap-paper angels from Blumchen.com
- 1 sheet 8½" x 11" (21.5cm x 28cm) pale blue card stock
- 1 package ¾"- (2cm-) wide medium size silver Lametta Tinsel wired fringe from Blumchen.com (you will only need about ¼ yd [23cm])
- 1 package 3mm-wide silver Steifkantille metal wire trim from Blumchen.com
- 21½" (54.5cm) Dresden edging trim (I purchased my medium-sized, silver, Frilly Fleuron Border at Blumchen.com—they come in packages of 10 strips)
- 1 package assorted Rococo Frames from Blumchen.com
- Double-sided tape

TOOLS

- Craft scissors
- Craft knife, self-healing cutting mat, and ruler
- Hot-glue gun

ARTWORK

- Scrap-paper angels clipart

INSTRUCTIONS

1 Cut out the star-shaped scrap-paper angel. Trace the star shape onto the pale blue card stock using a mechanical pencil and trim to size.

2 Curve 2–3" (5–7.5cm) of the silver Lametta Tinsel wired fringe into a circle shape and attach it to the back of the scrap-paper angel using a bead of glue from your hot-glue gun.

3 Cut six 3" (7.5cm) lengths of metal wire trim and curl them into spirals. Hot-glue the outer end of each spiral to the back of the scrap-paper angel, between the points of the star.

4 Hot-glue the light blue card stock star shape to the back of the ornament to hide the ends of the metal wire and fringe.

5 Cut out the oval-framed scrap-paper cherubs from Blumchen.com. With a mechanical pencil, trace the oval shape onto the sheet of light blue card stock using a mechanical pencil and trim to size.

tips

✦ Create more than one of each design to fill your tree. Simply scan in the artwork and print multiples of each paper design before assembling.

✦ Hang from traditional ornament hooks attached to the Lametta Tinsel or add a hole punch and silver grommet to the card stock to hang.

6 Curve another length of the silver Lametta Tinsel wired fringe into the oval shape and attach it along the perimeter of the back of the scrap-paper oval using a bead of glue from your hot-glue gun.

7 Hot-glue the light blue card stock oval to the back of the ornament to hide the ends of the fringe.

8 Cut out one of the smaller oval Rococo Frames and attach it to the front edges of the oval scrap-paper shape with a bead of glue from your hot-glue gun.

Holiday CD Favor

(Makes 1 Favor: 2 CD Labels and 1 Cover)

For a festive holiday send-off and a wonderful reminder of the season's best party, create a blend of quintessential holiday songs as a farewell gift. Package the magic of your holiday gathering in snowflake and sheet music details on the discs and cover. Guests will surely listen to it on their way home and for years to come!

MATERIALS

- 1 Avery Designpro Deluxe CD-ROM label-printing software disc
- 1 sheet CD/DVD labels (These labels come 2 sheets to a page; you will need one page per CD favor)
- 2 blank CDs (650 MB CD-R)
- 1 sheet 8½" x 11" (21.5cm x 28cm) white card stock
- 2 sheets Avery self-adhesive 9" x 12" (23cm x 30.5cm) laminating sheets
- 2 clear CD/DVD disc hubs (also called CD buttons or dots) with adhesive backing

TOOLS

- Craft knife, self-healing cutting mat, and ruler
- Bone folder

ARTWORK

- Vintage frame and snowflake clipart; authentic "Let It Snow" sheet music

INSTRUCTIONS

1 Load the Avery Designpro Deluxe CD-ROM label-printing software onto your computer and follow the instructions included to set up the file for your CD label design. Lay out 2 CD labels using scanned-in sheet music art, snowflake art, and fonts, and print onto the Avery label sheets following the enclosed instructions. Set "Disc 1" and "Disc 2" labels to distinguish the CDs.

2 Burn season-appropriate music tracks onto the CDs using your favorite music management or CD-burning software, peel off the labels' protective backing, and adhere CD labels onto each CD.

3 Create a 2-page 8½" x 11" (21.5cm x 28cm) document in your computer page layout or word-processing program and draw crop marks on each page (in the exact same location) for 2 sides of your CD cover that measure 10¼" (26cm) wide x 5" (12.5cm) high. Set crop marks on each page to score the document so that it folds in half to 5⅛" (13cm) wide x 5" (12.5cm)

high. Place the snowflake and frame artwork on page 1 inside the crop marks. Typeset the title, your name, and the date of the party on the front and the names of the song tracks on the back of the cover. Place the snowflake and frame artwork on page 2 inside the crop marks.

4 Print page 1 of the document on a sheet of white card stock. Flip the card over and print page 2 of the document on the back side.

5 Peel off the protective backing of one Avery self-adhesive laminating sheet and press onto the front of the card stock CD cover following the enclosed instructions. Press the remaining laminating sheet onto the back of the CD cover.

6 Trim your card to the crop marks. Use your bone folder to score and fold the cover in half crosswise.

7 Peel off the protective backing on 2 CD hubs and attach one to the center of each side of the inside cover.

New Year's Eve

Accordion-Fold Invitation 140

Guest Sign-In. 142

Resolution Reminder Card 142

Party Hat Menu. 144

Signature Drink Sign 146

Favor Tag 148

PARTIES COMMEMORATING THE NEW YEAR ARE THE OLDEST OF CELEBRATIONS, dating back four thousand years to the first celebrations in Babylon, which were held in early spring. New Year's Day was changed to January 1st about two thousand years ago, and Western civilization adopted the celebration of New Year's Eve in the 1600s. These days, New Year's Eve is often filled with overly indulgent partygoers, roadblocks, and crowds. Even casual local establishments have astronomical cover charges. For these and many other reasons—including safety!—the intimate at-home New Year's fete is the one I love the most. However and wherever you hold your party, you can use these design ideas to pamper your guests and usher in the new year with style.

Celebrating at home doesn't make a black-tie affair out of the question. On the contrary, there is something festive and fun about donning a gown or tuxedo to go absolutely nowhere! Invite guests to a grand affair with touches of whimsy. Make sure every aspect of your celebration has a black-and-white color scheme, beginning with the invitation. The most formal of color combinations, it adds unmistakable drama to your event. Take it a step further and request that your guests come dressed in black and white.

From the invitation to the guest sign-in, menu, favor tag, and signature drink sign, the fonts, colors, and imagery of this suite elicit the Roaring Twenties—when jazz, art deco, flappers, extravagant balls with live big-band music, dancing the Charleston at the Savoy, and breaking tradition were all the rage.

The Atmosphere

Punctuate all your black-and-white paperie and décor with stars, Swarovski crystals, and chandelier prisms to catch the light and create a glittery backdrop for your festivities. Mirrored mosaic tiles create a spectacular backdrop for your table setting. Consider using them as a bar surface, or glue them to circles of cork to make drink coasters. The tiles also make a dramatic cover for your guest sign-in book or votive candle-holders. The possibilities are endless. The outcome—fantastic!

London

Chicago ★ Houston

Denver ★ Phoenix

HAPPY NEW YEAR
AMY and TRAVIS
07 ★ 08

Los Angeles

Honolulu

Hosting Tips

Begin the celebration the moment guests arrive by greeting them at the door with a tray of small silver bells adorned with playful black and white ribbons. Affix tags with instructions to "ring in" the New Year at the stroke of midnight! If you have hired wait staff, serve the bells on butlered silver trays. Displaying them in a central location close to the coat check or refreshments earlier in the night will also ensure that everyone will see and pick up their bells in time to use them. You will be surprised how lovely and festive the random bell-ringing sounds throughout the night. Guests won't be able to resist testing the bells out well before the New Year!

Celebrate midnight over and over by having a countdown for each time zone. Set up a clock display and celebrate as cities around the world usher in the New Year. The bell ringing, kissing, and merriment can go on endlessly. Better still, if you have friends and family far away, it will remind you to call them when their clocks strike midnight.

Traditional New Year's foods are thought to bring luck. Many cultures believe that anything in the shape of a ring is portentous because it symbolizes "coming full circle," and completing a year's cycle. That's why you'll see the Dutch eating donuts on New Year's Day. So, at the end of a long evening, send your guests on their way with cups of hot cocoa and coffee garnished with mini donuts stacked on swizzle sticks!

Accordion-Fold Invitation

(Makes 1 Invitation)

Guests can't help but sense the excitement of the New Year when they receive this chic black-and-white accordion-fold invitation (also shown on page 137). Embellished with elaborate fonts and graphic stars and studded with shimmering crystals, the design is quirky yet ostentatious and conveys both sophistication and fun.

MATERIALS

- 1 sheet 11" x 17" (28cm x 43cm) white card stock
- 1 sheet 8½" x 11" (21.5cm x 28cm) white card stock
- Double-sided tape
- 1 sheet 8½" x 11" (21.5cm x 28cm) black card stock
- Twelve 2.8mm Swarovski flat-back hot-fix crystal rhinestones
- 1 sheet 8½" x 11" (21.5cm x 28cm) white crack-and-peel label stock
- 1 black A6 envelope (4¾" x 6½" [12cm x 16.5cm])

TOOLS

- Templates on page 158
- Craft knife, self-healing cutting mat, and ruler
- Bone folder
- Craft scissors
- Corner-rounding punch
- Hot-Fixer rhinestone setter

INSTRUCTIONS

1 For the accordion-fold portion of your invitation, create an 11" x 17" (28cm x 43cm) document and draw crop marks measuring 12.5" (32cm) wide x 4" (10cm) high. Place score marks at 3" (7.5cm), 6" (15cm), 9" (23cm), and 12" (30.5cm) to indicate where to place the card's folds. Set the type for your invitation.

2 Scan the star templates on page 158 and scatter small stars throughout the layout. Place large stars with their vertical centers at the 3" (7.5cm) and 9" (23cm) score marks. These will be cutout stars that pop up when the card is folded.

3 Print the document on the 11" x 17" (28cm x 43cm) white card stock. Trim the points of only

the right-hand side of each of the big stars at 3" (7.5cm) and 9" (23cm). Leave the left-hand side of the stars (everything left of the crop marks) intact. Score and fold the card at 3" (7.5cm), 6" (15cm), 9" (23cm), and 12" (30.5cm), being careful not to score through the centers of the big stars. Trim your card to the crop marks.

4 Create a 2-page 8½" x 11" (21.5cm x 28cm) document and draw crop marks for a card measuring 6" (15cm) wide x 4" (10cm) high on page 1. Set the type and scatter small stars throughout.

5 Print the document on the 8½" x 11" (21.5cm x 28cm) white card stock. Trim to the crop

marks. Round the top and bottom corners of the right side of the 6" x 4" (15cm x 10cm) card.

6 Attach the accordion-fold card to the flat card by applying a strip of double-sided tape on the front of the ½"- (13mm-) wide panel of the accordion-fold card, and adhere it to the back of the flat card on the left-hand side.

7 Apply double-sided tape to the back of the flat card on all four edges and attach it to the center of the sheet of 8½" x 11" (21.5cm x 28cm) black card stock. This will hide the seam created when the two cards were taped together.

8 Trim the black card stock to leave a ¼" (6mm) border on the top, bottom, and right-hand side of the flat card. Trim the left-hand side of the black card flush with the folded white card above. Round only the top and bottom corners of the right-hand side of the black card to match the rounded corners of the white card above.

9 Using the Hot-Fixer rhinestone setter, glue the Swarovski crystals to the centers of random stars throughout the invitation.

10 On page 2 of the document draw crop marks for a card measuring 5" (12.5cm) wide x 2½" (6.5cm) high for the mailing label. Set the type for your mailing label and scatter small stars throughout. (Up to 3 labels will fit on one 8½" x 11" [21.5cm x 28cm] page.)

11 Print the label on the sheet of 8½" x 11" (21.5cm x 28cm) white crack-and-peel label stock. Trim the label to the crop marks, peel off the backing, and adhere the label to the black A6 envelope.

---

tip

✦ Do not use crystals that are bigger than 4mm unless you are sending your invitation in a padded envelope or box. The larger the crystal, the more likely they will cause dents in the paper surrounding them after the invitation is run through the postal machines.

Guest Sign-In and Resolution Reminder Card

(Makes 3 Sign-In Cards, 1 Display Sign, and 1 Reminder Card)

Throw tradition (and your guest sign-in book) to the wind by asking your invitees to write their New Year's resolutions on custom cards. Months later, create a postcard mailer featuring a typographical treatment of all the resolutions, and send it to everyone as a whimsical reminder of their promises.

MATERIALS

- 3 sheets 8½" x 11" (21.5cm x 28cm) white card stock
- 1"- (2.5cm-) wide black-and-white diagonal stripe ribbon
- Glass bowl, jar, or vase
- 1 sheet 8½" x 11" (21.5cm x 28cm) black card stock
- Double-sided tape
- Three 2.8mm Swarovski flat-back hot-fix crystal rhinestones
- 2 clear wafer seals
- Decorative sign-in pens

TOOLS

- Templates on page 158
- 1" (2.5cm) hole punch
- Hot-glue gun
- Craft scissors
- Corner rounding punch
- Hot-Fixer rhinestone setter
- Craft knife, self-healing cutting mat, and ruler
- Bone folder

INSTRUCTIONS

1 Create a 3-page document measuring 8½" (21.5cm) wide x 11" (28cm) high. On the first page typeset each letter of the word "Resolutions" for the RESOLUTIONS sign in white inside a ⁹⁄₁₀" (2.3cm) black circle.

2 Print the document on a sheet of the white card stock. Using the 1" (2.5cm) hole punch, carefully punch out each letter. Be careful to center each black circle inside the hole punch to create a thin white border.

3 Cut the ribbon to fit down the side of your container and hot-glue it to the glass. Then hot-glue each circle onto the ribbon strip in a cascading pattern down the side of your container.

4 On the second page of the document, draw crop marks for 3 sign-in cards measuring 5" (12.5cm) wide x 3" (7.5cm). Set the type and small stars using the star templates on page 158.

Create a space for the guests' names and New Year's resolutions. Put a star next to the space for the name. Print the document on a sheet of white card stock. Trim to the crop marks.

5 Using the star templates on page 158 as a guide, lightly trace 1 medium star in pencil on the black card stock and cut it out with craft scissors. Use double-sided tape to affix it to the right-hand side of the resolutions card.

6 Cut the remaining black card stock to 5½" wide (14cm) x 3" (7.5cm) high. With the corner rounder, round the top left corner of both the black plain card and the white resolution card. Affix double-sided tape to the back of the white resolution card and attach it centered on the black card.

7 Using the Hot-Fixer rhinestone setter, glue a single crystal in the center of the tiny star next to the section for the guest's name.

8 On the third page of the document, draw crop marks for a card measuring 7" (18cm) wide x 8" (20.5cm) high for the Resolution Reminder Card. Draw crop marks or a solid frame around the entire document. Set the type and the stars. On the outside, lay out the return address and space for the guests' addresses. On the inside, include all of the resolutions written by your guests on New Year's Eve with an encouraging reminder to "Keep up the good work!"

9 Print the document on white card stock. Trim to the crop marks. Score and fold the card in half so the fold is at the top of the card. The folded size should be 7" (18cm) wide x 4" (10cm) high.

10 Seal with circular wafer seals at each end of the opening on the bottom of the folded mailer.

tip

✦ Do not use the crystals on the mailer design, as postal machines sometimes tear and dent the paper where the crystals are applied.

Party Hat Menu

(Makes 1 Party Hat)

Dinner menus that double as festive party hats will save on the table clutter and end-of-the-evening cleanup. Trimmed with crystals, stars, and ribbon streamers, no one will be able to resisting donning this gorgeous table decoration as the clock strikes twelve!

MATERIALS
- 1 sheet 11" x 17" (28cm x 43cm) text-weight white paper
- Spray mount
- 1 sheet 11" x 17" (28cm x 43cm) black card stock
- 15 2.8mm Swarovski flat-back hot-fix rhinestones
- Various black and white ¼"- (6mm-) and ⅛"- (3mm-) wide ribbons
- 40" (101.5cm) of ⅛"- (3mm-) thick black-and-white twisted rayon cord
- Two ⅛" (3mm) silver eyelets

TOOLS
- Template on page 159
- Craft scissors
- Craft knife, self-healing cutting mat, and ruler
- Pinking shears
- Hot-Fixer rhinestone setter
- ⅛" (3mm) hole punch
- Eyelet setter with self-healing mat and hammer
- Hot-glue gun

INSTRUCTIONS

1 Create a 17" (28cm) wide x 11" (43cm) high document. Place the Party Hat Menu template on page 159 onto your page, enlarged so that each side is 10" (25.5cm).

2 Set the type and rotate it 36.5 degrees counterclockwise so it fits within the scattered stars.

3 Print the card on the sheet of text-weight paper. Trim the left- and right-hand sides of the menu triangle along the template edges. Cut the entire curved bottom with pinking shears.

4 Spray the back of your menu with spray adhesive and attach it to the black card stock.

5 Trim the left- and right-hand sides of the black card stock flush with the edge of the menu. Cut the curved bottom of the black card stock with pinking shears, cutting it ¼" (6mm) larger than the menu to create a border. Use the rhinestone setter to glue crystals in the centers of the smallest stars.

6 Punch a hole on each side of the hat for the ties, 5" (12.5cm) from each side and ½" (13mm) from the bottom. Set the eyelets in the holes.

7 Curl/roll the menu into a cone shape, overlapping the sides slightly, and hot-glue it in place.

8 Snip the tip of the cone to create space for your ribbon streamers. The hole should be no larger than ¼" (13mm).

9 Cut the various ribbons into 12" (30.5cm) lengths and knot them together at one end. Thread the loose ends of the ribbons through the hole at the top and pull until the knot is at the top.

10 Cut the rayon cord into two 20" (51cm) lengths. Thread the cord through the holes on each side and tie a knot at the base to keep the cord from moving. Knot the ends to keep them from unraveling.

MENU

TEPPANYAKI GRILL

Beef, Chicken and Lamb Skewers
with Miso, Ponzu and Chili Sauces

Assorted Grilled Vegetables
in Olive Oil and Herbs

Hummus with Homemade Paprika Pita Chips

Vegetable Coconut Curry

LITTLE ITALY

Vegetarian Pesto

Penne Puttanesca

Beefsteak Tomatoes, Buffalo Mozzarella
Fresh Basil and Olive Oil Drizzle

Crab-stuffed Mushrooms

Mesclun Salad:
Smoked Lanai Venison, Maui Onion,
Red Peppers and Black Olives

SUNDAE BAR

Häagen-Dazs ice cream

Hot fudge, Marshmallow, Caramel, Bananas
Heath Bar, Oreo Cookies, Chocolate Chips
Whipped Cream and Cherries

Espresso, Cappuccino, Coffee, Tea

HAPPY NEW YEAR · 2008 · HAPPY NEW YEAR · 2008 · HAPPY NEW YEAR

Signature Drink Sign

(Makes 2 Signs)

Inspire guests to launch the New Year trying something novel. Display bar signs bursting with stars and shimmering crystals to show off sensational signature cocktails. Even the traditional libations feel more festive when you dream up fun names that reflect your New Year's party theme.

MATERIALS
- 1 sheet 8½" x 11" (21.5cm x 28cm) white card stock
- 2 sheets 8½" x 11" (21.5cm x 28cm) black card stock
- Double-sided tape
- Four 2.8mm Swarovski flat-back hot-fix crystal rhinestones

TOOLS
- Templates on page 158
- Craft scissors
- Craft knife, self-healing cutting mat, and ruler
- Corner rounding punch
- Hot-Fixer rhinestone setter
- ⅛" (3mm) hole punch
- Eyelet setter with self-healing mat and hammer

INSTRUCTIONS

1 Create a document in your computer page layout or word-processing program that is 8½" (21.5cm) wide x 11" (28cm) high. Draw crop marks for a card measuring 5" (12.5cm) wide x 4" (10cm) high. (You can fit up to 2 cards on an 8½" x 11" [21.5cm x 28cm] sheet.)

2 Set the type for your signature drink and scatter small stars throughout the layout using the star templates on page 158.

3 Print the card on the sheet of white card stock. Trim your card to size. Using the corner rounding punch, round all corners of the card.

4 Attach the card to one sheet of black card stock by applying double-sided tape to the back of the signature drink menu on all four edges of the card.

5 Trim the black card stock down so that it creates a ¼" (6mm) border on the top and right-hand sides of the white card and a ¾" (2cm)

border on the bottom and left-hand sides. Round all four corners of the black card to match the rounded corners of the white card.

6 Using the star templates on page 158 as a guide, lightly trace out 2 large stars and 2 medium stars in pencil on the second sheet of black card stock and cut them out with craft scissors.

7 Use double-sided tape to affix 2 black stars to each of the drink menus. Using the Hot-Fixer rhinestone setter, glue the Swarovski flat-back hot-fix crystals to the centers of random small stars throughout the menu.

8 Cut 2 pieces from the black card stock measuring 4" (10cm) wide x 7" (18cm) high and fold them in half to measure 4" (10cm) wide x 3½" (9cm) high.

9 Use double-sided tape to glue the folded card to the back of the drink signs in an upside-down V to create a tented stand.

ayan Resolution

OUNCE ⟡ ORGULLO TEQUILA

OUNCES ⟡ SOUR MIX

2 TABLESPOONS ⟡ FRESH RAS

1 OUNCE ⟡ CHAMPAGNE FLOAT

Midnight Nirvana

1 OUNCE ⟡ STOLI ORANGE VODKA

1 OUNCE ⟡ BLUE CURACAO

AND A SPLASH OF ⟡ SOUR MIX

TOPPED WITH ⟡ CHAMPAGNE

Favor Tag

(Makes 3 Favor Tags)

Give your guests a gift that they can use throughout the coming year, such as a calendar or daily planner with a matching pen. Or send your guests home with a gift they'll be sure to thank you for the next day: Create a "Hangover Kit" for each of your guests with bottled water, travel packets of Tylenol, an eye mask to block out the dreaded sun, Band-Aids for those cuts of mysterious origin that can appear after a great party, and a mini bottle of champagne for the "hair of the dog." Tuck them into shimmering silver glitter boxes filled with black crinkle paper complete with custom favor tags.

MATERIALS
- 1 sheet 8½" x 11" (21.5cm x 28cm) white card stock
- 2 sheets of 8½" x 11" (21.5cm x 28cm) black card stock
- Double-sided tape
- Three ⅛" (3mm) silver eyelets
- Striped grosgrain ribbon
- 2.8mm Swarovski flat-back hot-fix crystal rhinestones
- ¼"- (6mm) wide black-and-white striped grosgrain ribbon

TOOLS
- Templates on page 158
- 3" (7.5cm) hole punch
- Craft scissors
- Craft knife, self-healing cutting mat, and ruler
- Hot-Fixer rhinestone setter
- ⅛" (3mm) hole punch
- Eyelet setter with self-healing mat
- Hammer

INSTRUCTIONS

1 Create an 8½" (21.5cm) wide x 11" (28cm) high document in your computer page layout or word-processing program. Draw three 3⅛" (7.9cm) circular frames on the page. Place your logo and favor tag message inside each of these circles.

2 Print the document on the sheet of white card stock. Using the 3" (7.5cm) hole punch, carefully punch out the circular favor tag cards inside the circle frames. Punch out 6 more circles from one sheet of the black card stock.

3 Using the star templates on page 158 as a guide, lightly trace 3 large stars and 3 medium stars in pencil on the second sheet of black card stock and cut them out with craft scissors. Use

an art-gum eraser to remove any remaining pencil marks.

4 Use double-sided tape to affix 2 black circles, 1 black medium star, and 1 black large star to each white circular favor card.

5 Use the Hot-Fixer rhinestone setter to glue crystals in the centers of the smallest stars.

6 Create a hole at the top of each favor tag with the ⅛" (3mm) hole punch.

7 Using the eyelet setter with self-healing mat, reinforce the hole with a silver eyelet.

8 Cut the ¼"- (6mm-) wide ribbon to the lengths desired for your gift packages and thread one length through each card's eyelet hole.

Invitation Guidelines

GENERAL INVITATION GUIDELINES

When hosting an elegant affair, invitation wording is best when straightforward and not too kitschy, but it's always a great idea to add your own flair to personalize it. The key elements to remember when inviting your guests are the name of the event, who or what the event is celebrating, the date, time, host's name, location and address, RSVP instructions, and attire (if necessary).

Send one invitation per single guest, couple, or family. Though traditional business mailing labels are not acceptable for invitations of any kind, printing directly onto the outer envelope with a matching font is increasing in popularity and is an acceptable substitute for handwritten addresses. If you choose not to hire a professional calligrapher and cannot print directly onto your envelopes, computerized addressing on custom paper labels with matching fonts and decorative elements or borders is becoming more widely accepted. Be sure to send your invitations out a minimum of four weeks before your celebration date.

WEDDING INVITATION GUIDELINES

This section offers helpful suggestions and etiquette to guide you through creating your own wedding invitations.

Quantity

You will need one invitation per single guest, couple or family. It is also proper etiquette to send invitations to valued friends and relatives even if you know they will not be able to attend. If you are designing your invitations and sending them to a professional for printing, order an additional 15-25 invitations to allow for any addressing mistakes or last-minute additions to the guest list. Be sure to order invitations for your parents, in-laws, the officiant, and at least one for yourself as a keepsake. Print approximately 20 percent more envelopes for addressing mistakes and corrections. As long you make sure to send the second wave of invitations out at least four weeks before the wedding date, it is perfectly appropriate to have a "B" list when you find—as the response cards are returned—that you have room for a few more guests.

Timing

Mailing: Invitations should be mailed 6 to 8 weeks before your wedding date. If you have a large number of out-of-town guests, it is common courtesy to send them 8 to 10 weeks before, giving your guests time to make reservations and secure travel arrangements.

Calligraphy: Send envelopes and a final guest list to your calligrapher a minimum of 3 weeks before the mailing date.

RSVP: It is advisable to set the reply date 2 to 3 weeks before the event to allow time for the place cards and escort cards to be calligraphed and to give the caterer an accurate final head count. If any guests have not responded, it is perfectly acceptable to call them for their response. If they do not return your calls, assume they are coming. It is better to have food and a seat ready for them the day of your wedding than to be unprepared if they show up.

Save the Dates: If you are planning a destination wedding or getting married on a holiday or summer weekend, it is a good idea to send out a Save the Date announcement 6 to 8 months before the wedding to give your guests important information about travel, transportation, and hotels in the area.

Ordering: If you decide to design your invitations and send them to a professional for printing, be sure to order your invitations a minimum of 4 months before your wedding (6 months for custom designs), to allow for time to reprint if necessary.

WORDING GUIDELINES

- A traditional wedding invitation is made up of: a host line, a request line, bride and groom lines with a joining line ("to" or "and"), date and time lines, a location line, a location address line, a reception line, and an RSVP line.
- Using either spelling: "honor" or "honour" is appropriate as long as you format "favor" or "favour" the same way.
- "Request the honor ..." is reserved for weddings held on sanctified ground, "Request the pleasure ..." is used in all other circumstances.
- Initials are never properly used on a formal invitation card. It is better to omit the middle name entirely than to use the initial.
- Divorced parents should be listed on separate lines with the mother's name first.
- If the groom's parents are sharing the expenses, both sets of parents are listed with the bride's parents listed first.
- Though step parents can be included, when either of the bride's parents have remarried, it is most proper to list only the natural parents.

- To include everyone, the couple can invite the guests themselves, and either mention both families or preface their names on the host line with "Together with their families ..."
- When the time of day is unclear, specify "in the morning" or "in the evening."
- To specify a ceremony on the half hour, "At half after six o'clock" should be used for formal wedding celebrations and "at six-thirty" can be used for a less formal affair.
- When stating the time, it is not necessary to specify a.m. or p.m. The hour is sufficient.
- If the ceremony and reception are at the same location, it is not necessary to enclose a separate card. Simply write, "and afterward at the reception," at the bottom of the invitation.
- It is only necessary to mention the reception start time if the reception does not immediately follow the ceremony.
- You should include a street address for any location that is not well known.
- The most formal RSVP is handwritten by the guest on their own stationery. If you choose this option, the word RSVP is printed in the bottom left corner of the invitation card. The most common and convenient way to have guests reply is to include an RSVP card with a self-addressed, stamped return envelope. The postcard RSVP is the most contemporary and casual method for guest responses.
- It is never appropriate to request that guests respond via phone or fax. Responses to wedding invitations should be handwritten.
- It is never appropriate to mention that children are not invited except by word of mouth.
- It is never appropriate to mention your gift registry anywhere on your invitation. You may mention it in the bridal shower invitation, on your wedding website, or by word of mouth.
- It is never appropriate to request that guests send a donation to your favorite charity in lieu of gifts. You should expect nothing except the pleasure of their company. However, it is perfectly acceptable to make a charitable donation on behalf of your guests in lieu of giving favors.

Wording Etiquette

Though your wording should reflect the style and the formality of your wedding, it is best to use your own judgment and do what makes you feel most comfortable.

Sample Wording

Bride's Married Parents Hosting (Traditional Wording)
Mr. and Mrs. John Michael Smith
request the honor of your presence
at the marriage of their daughter
Amy Elizabeth
to
Mr. Joseph Allen Jones
Saturday, the twenty-fifth of April
Two thousand and nine
at one o'clock in the afternoon
The Old South Church
Boston, Massachusetts

One of Bride's Parents Is Deceased
Mr. John Michael Jones
requests the honor of your presence
at the marriage of his daughter
Amy Elizabeth
or
Amy Elizabeth Jones
daughter
of Beth Anne Jones
and
John Michael Jones and
James Frank Smith
son of
Mr. and Mrs. Robert James Smith

request the honor of your presence
at their marriage

Couple Hosts
The honor of your presence
is requested at the marriage of
Miss Amy Elizabeth Jones
to
Mr. James Frank Smith
or
Amy Elizabeth Jones and
James Frank Smith
request the honor of your presence
at their marriage

Bride's Divorced Parents Host
Mrs. James Frank Smith [mother]
and
Mr. Robert Allen Jones [father]
request the pleasure of your company
at the wedding of their daughter
Amy Elizabeth Jones
or
Mr. and Mrs. James Frank Smith
[mother and husband] and
Mr. and Mrs. Robert Allen
Jones [father and wife]
request the pleasure of your company
at the marriage of Amy Elizabeth

Bride's Remarried Mother Hosts, Father Deceased
Mr. and Mrs. John Michael Smith
request the honor of your presence
at the marriage of her daughter
Amy Elizabeth Jones
daughter of Robert Allen Jones

Bride's Widowed Parent Hosts
Mr./Mrs. John Michael Smith
request the honor of your presence
at the marriage of his/her daughter
Amy Elizabeth Smith

Groom's Married Parents Hosting
Mr. and Mrs. Robert James Smith
request the honor of your presence
at the marriage of
Miss Amy Elizabeth Jones
to their son
James Frank Smith

Both Bride and Groom's Parents Host
Mr. and Mrs. John Michael Smith
and
Mr. and Mrs. Robert James Smith
request the honor of your presence
at the marriage of their children

Reception Card
Reception immediately following the
ceremony

State Room
Sixty State Street, Boston
or
A celebration will follow in the spirit of
love, laughter, and happily ever after
State Room
Sixty State Street, Boston

Response Card
M _____
will _____ attend
The favor of a reply is requested
before the third of April
or
M _____
_____ will attend _____ will not attend
The favor of a reply is requested
before the third of April
or
M _____
_____ joyfully accepts _____ regretfully
declines
The favor of a reply is requested
before the third of April
or
M _____
_____ accepts _____ regrets
The favor of a reply is requested
before the third of April

elements of paperie suite

The Invitation
- Outer and inner mailing envelopes (lined or unlined) or a mailing box and label
- Invitation card
- RSVP card and envelope or RSVP postcard
- Map/directions/travel cards
- Weekend events or itinerary card
- Separate reception card

Additional wedding-specific invitation cards: within the ribbon card and at home cards

The Paperie Suite
- Save the dates
- Invitations
- Informational mailers
- Welcome notes
- Custom water bottle labels
- Custom maps
- Ceremony or event programs
- Guest sign-in (book, cards, etc.)
- Cocktail napkins and restroom hand towels or coasters
- Escort cards (also known as seating cards; they direct guests to their tables)
- Table markers

- Place cards (positioned at each place setting)
- Menus
- Favor or gift tags
- Thank-you notes
- Personal stationery

Other items to consider: rehearsal dinner invitation, door knockers, buffet signs, event signage to direct guests to the site, custom gift wrap and tissue paper

Additional wedding-specific designs to consider: rehearsal dinner and brunch invitations added to the invitation design to save on postage costs

CALLIGRAPHY

Addresses on wedding invitation envelopes should be handwritten. It is perfectly acceptable to write the addresses yourself, but if you choose to hire a professional calligrapher, here are some valuable tips to ensure a smooth process with minimal errors. Submit your guest list in 12-point type in alphabetical order by last name. There should be only one column of addresses per page. Addresses should be numbered for easy referencing and proofing. Finally, all names and addresses should be typed exactly as you would like them to appear on both the inner and outer envelopes.

ADDRESSING

A guest's social or professional title, full name, and address is written on the face of the outer envelope. The name of the guest is then repeated on the inner using only their title and last name (for less formal occasions, first names are acceptable on the inner envelopes). The inner envelope is also reserved for the first names of children under eighteen, if they are invited, and the words, "and guest," for single invitees, both of which should not be on the outer envelope. If you choose to send your invitations in a box or a single outer envelope, names of all invitees should be listed on the label or envelope.

Nicknames or abbreviations should be avoided whenever possible except for Mr., Mrs., Jr., etc. Cities, states, and numbered streets are written out in full (with the exception of Washington D.C.). Numerals are used for house numbers. However, it is appropriate to write out numbers one through twenty. Numbered streets may be written whichever way looks more aesthetically pleasing. The only optional abbreviations when addressing are for Saint (St.), or Mount (Mt.), both of which can be written either way.

Tip: Address envelopes like a pro. Before you line your envelopes, trim a piece of paper to fit inside them. Using a ruler and a black permanent marker, draw four to five evenly spaced lines parallel to the bottom of the paper. Insert your guide into the envelope, and you'll have a guide to guarantee straight lines. For best results, place the envelope on a light table (you can create one at home by placing a desk lamp with the shade removed under a glass table), and the lines will show through all but the darkest envelopes.

Variations in Addressing:

Couples

- When a woman who is married has kept her maiden name she is listed first with the title "Mrs."

- Invitations to unmarried couples not living together should be sent to whomever is your closest friend.
- Unmarried couples who live together should be listed alphabetically by last name.
- Same-gender couples should be listed alphabetically by last name.

Children

- Children over 18 should receive their own invitation, even if they are still living at home.

Judges

Outer: The Honorable and Mrs. John Smith
Inner: Judge and Mrs. Smith

Doctors

Married Couple, Both Doctors
Outer: Doctors John and Jane Smith
Inner: The Doctors Smith

- When sending to a medical doctor, the word "Doctor" is spelled out. If the doctor is a PhD, the abbreviation "Dr." is used.
- When using her professional title, a married woman doctor is listed before her husband.

ENVELOPE SIZE CHART

Below you will find the measurements for the most widely used correspondence envelopes and their inserts.

Mini-lope or Escort Card Envelope

Size	Envelope	Insert card
	2 1/8" x 3 5/8" (5.5cm x 9.2cm)	2" x 3 1/4" (5cm x 8.2cm)

Baronial

Size	Envelope	Insert card
4-bar	3 5/8" x 5 1/8" (9.2cm x 13cm)	3 1/2" x 4 7/8" (9cm x 12cm)
5-bar	4 1/8" x 5 5/8" (10.5cm x 14.3cm)	4" x 5 3/8" (10.2cm x 13.7cm)
6-bar	4 3/4" x 6 1/2" (12cm x 16.5cm)	4 5/8" x 6 1/4" (11.7cm x 15.9cm)
Lee	5 1/4" x 7 1/4" (13.3cm x 18.5cm)	5" x 7" (12.5cm x 18cm)

Announcement

Size	Envelope	Insert card
A2	4 3/8" x 5 3/4" (11cm x 14.6cm)	4 1/4" x 5 1/2" (11cm x 14cm)
A6	4 3/4" x 6 1/2" (12cm x 16.5cm)	4 1/2" x 6" (11.5cm x 15cm)
A7	5 1/4" x 7 1/4" (13.3cm x 18.5cm)	5 x 7" (12.5cm x 18cm)
A8	5 1/2" x 8 1/4" (14cm x 21cm)	5 1/4" x 7 7/8" (13.3cm x 20cm)
A9	5 3/4" x 8 3/4" (14.5cm x 22cm)	5 1/2" x 8 1/2" (14cm x 21.5cm)
A10	6" x 9 1/2" (15cm x 24cm)	5 3/4" x 9 1/4" (14.5cm x 23.5cm)

Square

Size	Envelope	Insert card
5 3/4	5 3/4" x 5 3/4" (14.6cm x 14.6cm)	5 1/2" x 5 1/2" (14cm x 14cm)
6 1/2	6 1/2" x 6 1/2" (16.5cm x 16.5cm)	6 1/4" x 6 1/4" (16cm x 16cm)

Business

Size	Envelope	Insert card
#10	4 1/8" x 9 1/2" (10.5cm x 24cm)	3 7/8" x 9 1/4" (10cm x 23.5cm)
#10	Commercial has a shallow pointed flap on the long edge.	
#10	Square has a shallow rectangular flap on the long edge.	
#10	Policy, also called #10 Open End, has a rectangular flap on the short edge and is the most elegant of the #10 Business envelopes	

Catalog

Size	Envelope	Insert card
	9" x 12" (23cm x 30.5cm)	8 1/2" x 11 1/2" (21.5cm x 29.2cm)

Resources

The contact information in this section will lead you to some of my favorite vendors and suppliers. Though I have provided additional resources for the more adventurous readers, all projects featured in this book were created using products and materials from the vendors listed here. For more inspiration and design ideas please visit the Grapevine website, grapevinepaperie.com. Enjoy!

ANTIQUES & COLLECTIBLES

Ebay.com
The best online source for vintage postcards, ephemera, antiques, and collectibles

The Brimfield Fair
brimfield.com
Brimfield, Massachusetts
Vintage postcards, ephemera, antiques, collectibles

New York City Antiques
hellskitchenfleamarket.com
The Annex/Hell's Kitchen Flea Market, The West 25th Street Market, and The Antiques Garage
Open each weekend, the markets hold hundreds of vendors selling eclectic antiques, collectibles, vintage items, and decorative arts from all eras

Les Puces de Saint-Ouen
Paris, France
Metro stop: Porte de Clignancourt on Saturday, Sunday, or Monday
Antiques and flea market finds. More than two thousand vendors selling everything from chandeliers to buttons, etchings, photographs, clocks, Paris street signs, tapestries, and watches

ART-TISSUE™ HEARTS

Caufield's Novelty, Inc.
caufields.com
(800) 777-5653

Partycheap.com
partycheap.com
(800) 224-3143

ARTWORK

D. Blumchen & Company
blumchen.com
Scrap paper pictures, vintage artwork, Dresden trims

Stampington & Company
stampington.com
(877) STAMPER
Scrap paper pictures, vintage artwork, rubber stamps, scrapbooking supplies, decorative metal frames and hangers

Dover Publications
doverpublications.com
A great source for artwork, both vintage and modern, including clipart, patterns, illustrations, bookplates, monograms, postcards, and ephemera. Many of their books come with CDs of the artwork, but some have images that need to be scanned before using

Clipart.com
Medium resolution artwork that can be downloaded endlessly for a minimal weekly, monthly, or yearly fee

flickr.com
Millions of black-and-white and color photographs categorized and shared by people all over the world. Many are copyright-free, but ask permission before using

Shutterstock.com
Royalty-free stock photos for commercial and personal use. Less than one dollar per image with a month's subscription. Some of the designs and photos are really worth it!

BOXES & PACKAGING

Mason Box Company
masonbox.com
(800) 225-2708

Paper Mart
Papermart.com
(800) 745-8800

Paper Source
paper-source.com
(888) PAPER-11
5" x 7" (12.5cm x 18cm) invitation mailers in colors to match their card stock and envelopes

U.S. Box Corp
USbox.com
(800) 221-0999

CALLIGRAPHY

Larry Orlando
(featured calligrapher—Wedding)
larryorlando.com
Calligraphy and monograms
For a list of talented calligraphers in your state, visit cynscribe.com/usascribes.html

CONFETTI

Ecoparti
Ecoparti.com
(877) 473-8257
100 percent biodegradable and water soluble confetti with no cleanup. Available in a multitude of colors for your bridal tossing cones!

Save on Crafts
Save-on-crafts.com
(831) 768-8428
Dried lavender buds at bulk discount prices

CRAFT TOOLS & SUPPLIES

The Binding Source
bindingsource.com
Scotch ATG double-sided tape gun and tape cartridges, CD hubs/buttons, glue dots and adhesives

IKEA
Visit ikea.com to order online or to find a store in your area.
Affordable workspace organization containers and storage containers and supplies

LetterSeals.com
letterseals.com
Wax seals and glue-gun sealing wax

Martha Stewart Crafts
marthastewartcrafts.com
Tools, embellishments, adhesives, hole punches, and craft essentials

Michaels Stores, Inc.
Visit michaels.com to find a store in your area.
Art and craft supplies like corner rounding punches and dowel caps, scrapbooking, framing, paper, adhesives, Making Memories supplies, Martha Stewart Crafts, and more

Making Memories
makingmemories.com
Crafting tools and materials

WoodCrafter.com
woodcrafter.com
Dowel caps

DÉCOR & INTERIORS

Ballard Designs
ballarddesigns.com

Barnard, Ltd.
barnardltd.com

eBay
eBay.com

Home Goods
homegoods.com

Lamplight Feather
lamplightfeather.net

LightBulbsDirect.com
25-watt soft pink, amber, and soft white light bulbs

Pier 1 Imports
pier1.com
(800) 245-4595

Plum Party
PlumParty.com
(800) 227-0314
Tissue-paper grass mat (Outdoor Fete)

Target
target.com
(800) 591-3869

TN Farm Supply
tnfarmsupply.com
4½" (11.5cm) round Jiffy Peat Pot #340 Small
Quantities (25 ct.)

Wisteria
wisteria.com
2055 Luna Road, Suite 182
Carrollton, TX 75006
(800) 320-9757

EMBELLISHMENTS

D. Blümchen & Company
Blumchen.com
(866) OLD-XMAS
Gold rococo frames and gold fleuron border for
the Scrapbook Invitation (Anniversary)

M&J Trimming
mjtrim.com
1008 6th Avenue (between 37th and 38th Streets)
New York, NY 10018
(800) 9-MJTRIM
Ribbons, crystals, buttons, buckles, trims and tassels from around the world

Joyce Trimming Inc.
Ejoyce.com
(800) 719-7133
Ribbons, crystals, buttons, buckles, trims and
tassels

Trims Plus
Trimsplus.com
(909) 337-7705
Cotton ball fringe and mini ball fringe trim

FONTS

Dafont.com

Fonts.com

Myfonts.com

Urbanfonts.com

GRAPEVINE

grapevinepaperie.com
Silver and brass decorative bells, silk-covered
folding easels (Wedding Table Markers), vintage
reproduction *milagros* (Wedding Custom Gift Tags)
vintage postcard art (Wedding Save the Date and
Postcard Sign-In, Holiday Songbook Invitation)

PAPER & ENVELOPES

Envelope Mall
envelopemall.com
238 N Oakley Blvd
Chicago IL 60612
(800) 632-4242
Glassine envelopes for the Lottery Ticket Favor
(Anniversary). 100 per pack

Michaels
michaels.com
8000 Bent Branch Dr.
Irving, TX 75063
(800) MICHAELS

Paper and More
paperandmore.com
11" x 17" (28cm x 43cm) 29-lb translucent vellum
paper. They will cut your paper order to size upon
request

Paper Source
paper-source.com
(888) PAPER-11
Matching envelopes, card stock, and text-weight
paper in a wide array of colors and sizes with
ribbon to match. A great source for Incredi Tape,
book cloth, glitter, rubber stamps, wax seals and
glue gun sealing wax, mailing boxes, and more

Paper-Papers
paper-papers.com
An extensive selection of envelopes with card
stock and text-weight paper to match. They will
cut your paper order to size upon request

Creative Papers Online
handmade-paper.us
(800) 727-3740
Huge selection of handmade paper and card stock
from around the world. Large sheets of translucent vellum

Talas
talasonline.com
20 West 20th Street
New York, NY 10011
(212) 219-0770
Cork paper, silk book cloth, bookbinding supplies

POSTAGE

Champion Stamp Company Inc.
championstamp.com
432 West 54th Street
New York, N.Y. 10019
(212) 489-8130
The number one resource for ordering large
quantities of vintage, out of print stamps for your
invitation designs

Zazzle
Zazzle.com
(888) 8ZAZZLE
The best online resource for designing and creating personalized custom postage stamps, stickers,
buttons, T-shirts, gift bags, posters, and more

RUBBER STAMPS

Logan Stamp Works, Inc.
loganstamp.com
(800) 538-3232
Custom rubber stamp creation from your personal
artwork

SCREW POST BINDING

Screwpost.com
screwpost.com
(800) 808-2377
⅛" (3mm) gold-coated aluminum screw posts
(also available in silver and many other sizes)

SILK & FABRIC

Fabric.com
fabric.com
(888) 455-2940
Silk dupioni fabric in a wide array of colors

Joann Fabric and Craft Stores
joann.com
5555 Darrow Rd.
Hudson, OH 44236
(888) 739-4120
Scrim and netting, yarn, and textiles

Zimmans
zimmans.com
260 Lynnway, Rt. 1A
Lynn, MA 01901
(781) 598-9432

Artwork Sources

PERSONAL STATIONERY
Font used: Din Pro

Business Card: Monogram art from Dover Publications

Letterhead and Overlay: Butterfly art from a vintage book and Monogram Art from Dover Publications. Mailing Labels: Butterfly art from a vintage book and Monogram Art from Dover Publications

#10 Business Envelope: Monogram Art from Dover Publications

Fold-Over Note Card: Monogram art from Dover Publications

Flat Note Card: Butterfly from vintage book and Monogram Art from Dover Publications

DINNER PARTY
Fonts used: Frisco Antique Display, Inspiration, Frutiger, and Saddlery Fill

The Invitation: Pattern and frame artwork from Dover Publications. Photographs of Paris from Flickr.com. Vintage map of Paris from my own collection

Guest Sign-In Map: Vintage map of Paris from my own collection. (Mine came from the Paris flea markets, but an online search yields many choices.)

Pocket Escort Cards: Pattern and frame artwork from Dover Publications

Table Markers: Eiffel Tower postcard sticker from Cavallini.com; Paris stickers in a tin purchased at PaperSource.com

Menus: Pattern artwork from Dover Publications

Soap Label Favor Gift Wrap: Pattern and frame artwork from Dover Publications

OUTDOOR FETE
Fonts used: Adobe Jenson and Virginia Antique

The Invitation: Citrus illustrations from Clipart.com; decorative frame artwork from Dover Publications

Signature Drink Sign and Tags: Citrus illustrations from Clipart.com; decorative frame artwork from Dover Publications

Utensil Display: Citrus illustrations from Clipart.com; decorative frame artwork from Dover Publications

Menu Paddle Fan: Citrus illustrations from Clipart.com; decorative frame artwork from Dover Publications

WINE TASTING
Fonts used: Din Pro, Mrs. Eaves Roman, and Ellida

Gate-Fold Invitation: Crown and vintage ornamental rules from Dover Publications. The orange frame around the entire invitation and label are standard picture-box frames found in my layout program.

Tasting Notes: Vintage map from antique shop

Wine-Tasting Program Kiosk: Crown and vintage ornamental rules from Dover Publications

Reminder Postcard: Crown and vintage ornamental rules from Dover Publications

Drink Coasters: Crown from Dover Publications and vintage map from antique shop

Wine-Glass Tags: Crown and vintage ornamental rules from Dover Publications

THE OSCARS
Fonts used: Brittanic Bold, Adobe Garamond, and Gloria Script

Shadow Box Invitation: Ribbon banners, stars, art deco border, and burst from Dover Publications. Camera from Clipart.com.

Oscar Ballots: Ribbon banners from Dover Publications

Trivia Fans: Ribbon banners from Dover Publications

Treat Cones: Movie artwork from posters I have purchased

BIRTHDAY
Font used: Baskerville

ANNIVERSARY
Fonts used: University Script, Gloucester, Smackeroo, Adobe Garamond, Times, and Frutiger

WEDDING
Fonts used: Adobe Garamond

Postcard Guest Sign-In: Vintage postcards from eBay.com and antiques fairs

Save the Date: Vintage postcard art (available at grapevinepaperie.com)

Postcard Sign-in: Vintage postcard art (available at grapevinepaperie.com)

All Other Projects: Custom calligraphy by Larry Orlando

HOLIDAY GATHERING
Fonts used: Chappel Text, Adobe Jenson, Academy Engraved, and CgLiberty

Songbook Invitation: Vintage snowflake artwork from Dover Publications, vintage postcard art from my own collection, and authentic "Let It Snow" sheet music from eBay.com

Wish Tree Sign-In: Vintage frame artwork from Dover Publications and vintage postcard art from my own collection

Holiday Recipe Stocking Stuffer: Vintage frame artwork from Dover Publications and vintage postcard art from my own collection

Scrap-Paper and Tinsel Ornaments: Scrap-paper angels artwork from Blumchen.com

Holiday CD Favor: Vintage frame and snowflake artwork from Dover Publications and authentic "Let It Snow" sheet music from eBay.com

NEW YEAR'S EVE
Fonts used: Zinc Italian, Zapf Dingbats, Mazurka, and DIN

Templates

CREATING CROP MARKS

Also known as "corner marks" or "margin marks," crop marks are much like the crosshairs in a rifle scope. They are composed of 2 small lines positioned at a 90 degree angle and placed at the corners of an image or a page to indicate where to trim and eliminate unprinted or unneeded portions of your page. They may be drawn on manually or automatically applied with some desktop publishing software programs like Microsoft Publisher, Adobe InDesign, Adobe Illustrator, Adobe Pagemaker, and Quark Xpress. If you do not own or are not familiar with these layout programs, I suggest using Microsoft PowerPoint for all of your paperie suite designs. It offers a great deal of flexibility in placement of text, graphics, and frames.

How to draw crop marks
(see Template below to illustrate this exercise):

1 Create a single crop mark (two lines or rules with a 1 point width placed at a right angle) in the top left corner of your design. Keep crop marks approximately $\frac{1}{8}$" (3mm) from the edge of your page.

2 Group the crop mark, and copy and paste it. Then rotate the resulting object 90 degrees and move it to the top right corner.

3 Copy and paste the second crop mark and rotate the resulting object 90 degrees for the bottom right corner.

4 Copy and paste the third crop mark and rotate the resulting object 90 degrees. Move it to the bottom left corner.

Be sure your crop marks fall inside the printable area. If you use a page layout program, manually drawing crop marks will not be necessary. Simply create the document at actual size and check the box to "print with crop or registration marks" in your print window. When creating multiple designs or cards on a single document page, use guides to mark the edges of your designs and ensure proper placement of artwork within the crop marks.

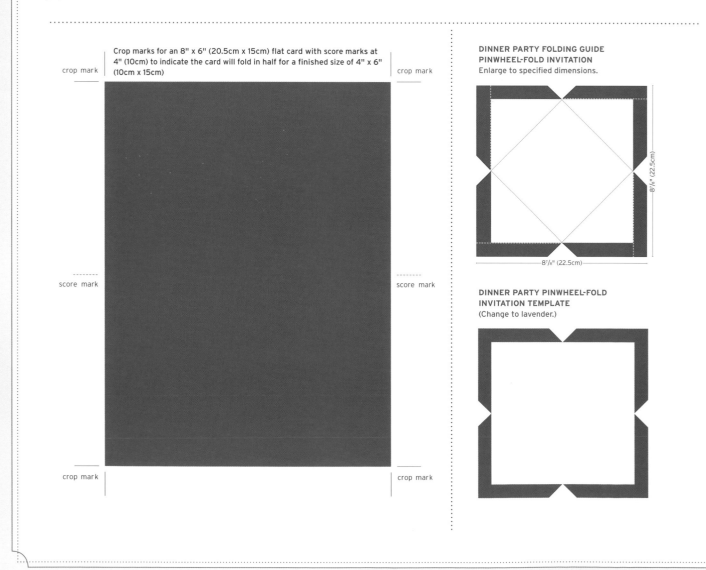

crop mark

Crop marks for an 8" x 6" (20.5cm x 15cm) flat card with score marks at 4" (10cm) to indicate the card will fold in half for a finished size of 4" x 6" (10cm x 15cm)

crop mark

score mark

score mark

crop mark

crop mark

DINNER PARTY FOLDING GUIDE PINWHEEL-FOLD INVITATION
Enlarge to specified dimensions.

8⁷/₈" (22.5cm)

8⁷/₈" (22.5cm)

DINNER PARTY PINWHEEL-FOLD INVITATION TEMPLATE
(Change to lavender.)

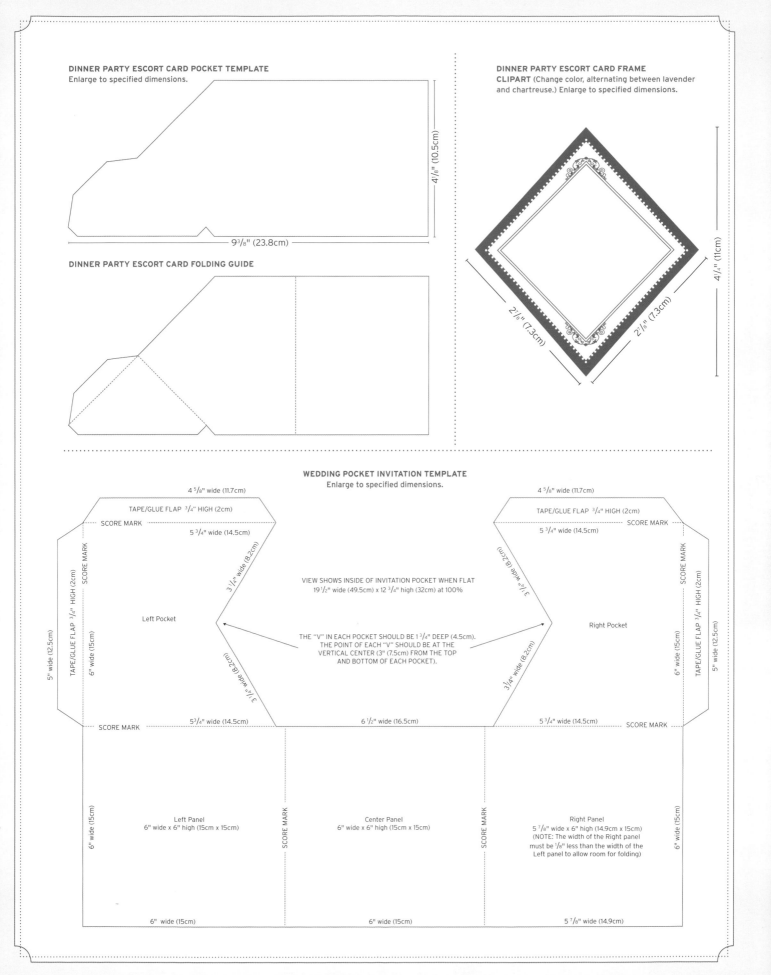

DINNER PARTY ESCORT CARD POCKET TEMPLATE
Enlarge to specified dimensions.

4 1/8" (10.5cm)

9 3/8" (23.8cm)

DINNER PARTY ESCORT CARD FOLDING GUIDE

DINNER PARTY ESCORT CARD FRAME
CLIPART (Change color, alternating between lavender and chartreuse.) Enlarge to specified dimensions.

4 1/4" (11cm)

2 7/8" (7.3cm)

2 7/8" (7.3cm)

WEDDING POCKET INVITATION TEMPLATE
Enlarge to specified dimensions.

4 5/8" wide (11.7cm)

TAPE/GLUE FLAP 3/4" HIGH (2cm)

SCORE MARK

5 3/4" wide (14.5cm)

SCORE MARK

TAPE/GLUE FLAP 3/4" HIGH (2cm)

3 1/4" wide (8.2cm)

Left Pocket

VIEW SHOWS INSIDE OF INVITATION POCKET WHEN FLAT
19 1/2" wide (49.5cm) x 12 3/4" high (32cm) at 100%

THE "V" IN EACH POCKET SHOULD BE 1 3/4" DEEP (4.5cm).
THE POINT OF EACH "V" SHOULD BE AT THE
VERTICAL CENTER (3" (7.5cm) FROM THE TOP
AND BOTTOM OF EACH POCKET).

Right Pocket

3 1/4" wide (8.2cm)

6" wide (15cm)

5" wide (12.5cm)

3 1/4" wide (8.2cm)

SCORE MARK

5 3/4" wide (14.5cm)

6 1/2" wide (16.5cm)

5 3/4" wide (14.5cm)

SCORE MARK

6" wide (15cm)

Left Panel
6" wide x 6" high (15cm x 15cm)

SCORE MARK

Center Panel
6" wide x 6" high (15cm x 15cm)

SCORE MARK

Right Panel
5 7/8" wide x 6" high (14.9cm x 15cm)
(NOTE: The width of the Right panel
must be 1/8" less than the width of the
Left panel to allow room for folding)

6" wide (15cm)

6" wide (15cm)

6" wide (15cm)

5 7/8" wide (14.9cm)

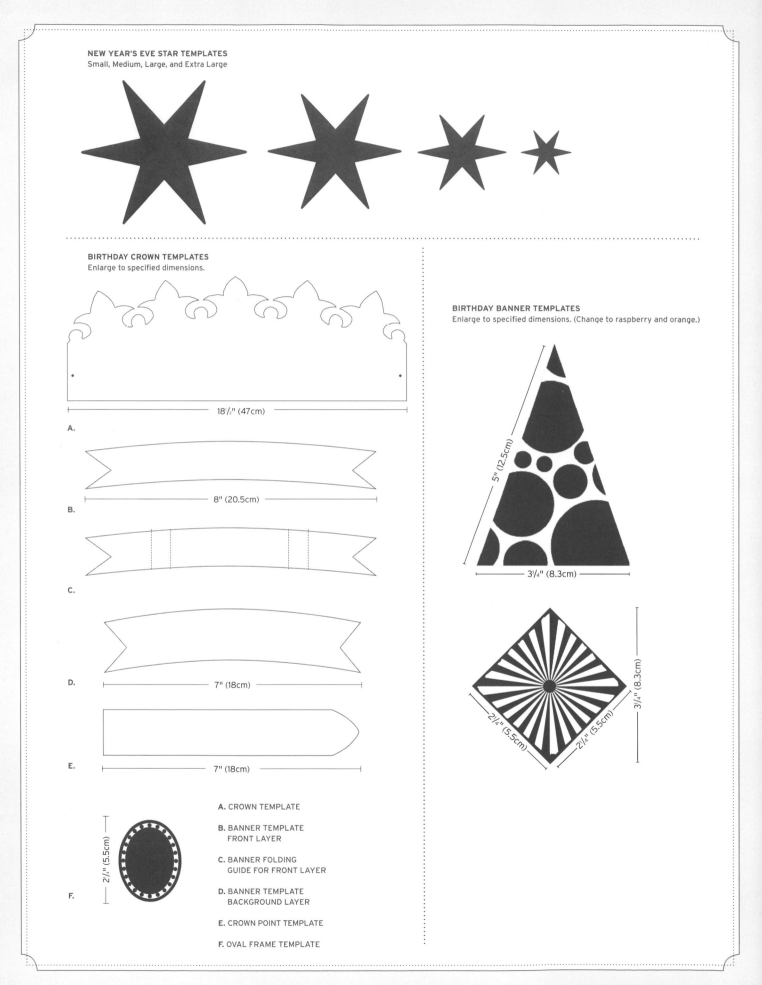

NEW YEAR'S EVE STAR TEMPLATES
Small, Medium, Large, and Extra Large

BIRTHDAY CROWN TEMPLATES
Enlarge to specified dimensions.

18 1/2" (47cm)

A.

8" (20.5cm)

B.

C.

7" (18cm)

D.

7" (18cm)

E.

2 1/4" (5.5cm)

F.

A. CROWN TEMPLATE

B. BANNER TEMPLATE
FRONT LAYER

C. BANNER FOLDING
GUIDE FOR FRONT LAYER

D. BANNER TEMPLATE
BACKGROUND LAYER

E. CROWN POINT TEMPLATE

F. OVAL FRAME TEMPLATE

BIRTHDAY BANNER TEMPLATES
Enlarge to specified dimensions. (Change to raspberry and orange.)

5" (12.5cm)

3 1/4" (8.3cm)

2 1/4" (5.5cm)

2 1/4" (5.5cm)

3 1/4" (8.3cm)

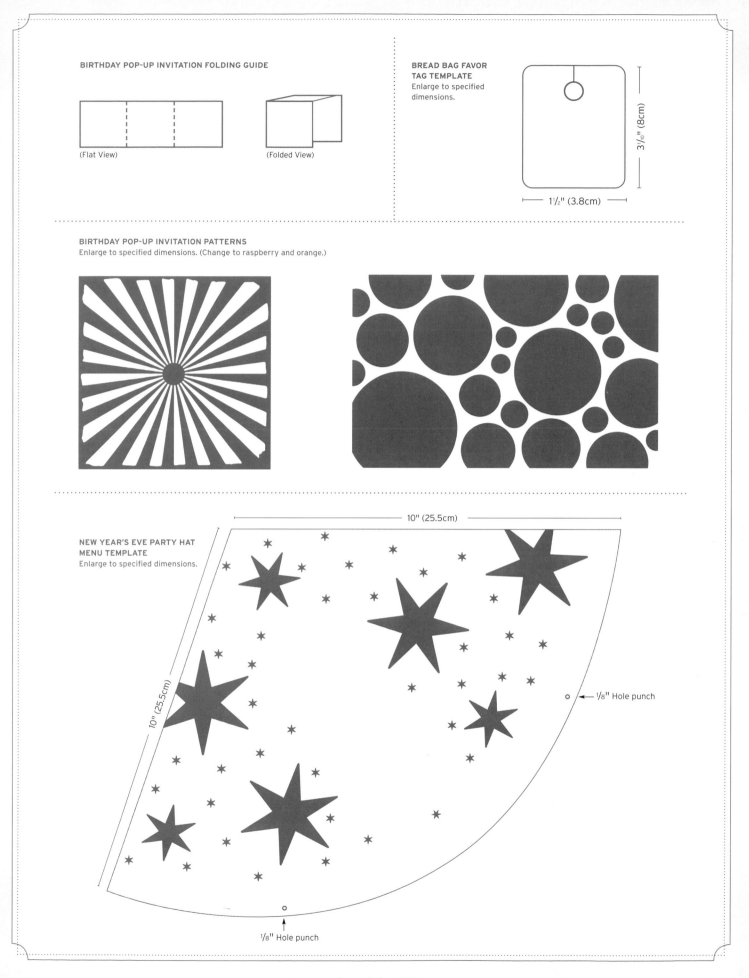

BIRTHDAY POP-UP INVITATION FOLDING GUIDE

(Flat View)

(Folded View)

BREAD BAG FAVOR TAG TEMPLATE
Enlarge to specified dimensions.

3¹/₁₀" (8cm)

1½" (3.8cm)

BIRTHDAY POP-UP INVITATION PATTERNS
Enlarge to specified dimensions. (Change to raspberry and orange.)

NEW YEAR'S EVE PARTY HAT MENU TEMPLATE
Enlarge to specified dimensions.

10" (25.5cm)

10" (25.5cm)

⅛" Hole punch

⅛" Hole punch

Index

Academy Awards (Oscars)
cocktail drinks for, 70
hosting tips, 70
Oscar ballot, 73
shadow box invitation, 71–72
treat cone, 76–77
trivia fan, 74–75
Accordion-fold invitation, 140–141
Anniversary
anniversary herald, 96,
100–101
custom cocktail napkins, 97
hosting tips, 96
lottery ticket favor, 102–103
pocket scrapbook invitation,
98–99
Anniversary herald, 100–101

Basic adhesives, 6
Basic materials, 6
Basic tools, 6
Birthday
birthday banner and timeline,
88–89
birthday crown, 84–87
circle menu, 92–93
hosting tips, 80
pop-up invitation, 82–83
surprise-party face masks,
90–91
Birthday banner and timeline,
88–89
Birthday crown, 84–87
Blind tasting bottle cover, 62–63
Bread bag favor tag, 52–53
Business card, 20

Calligraphy, 152
Candy cane cocoa, 129
Circle menu, 92–93
Color scheme, choosing of, 9
Creative design
form vs. function, 9
invitation, 8
process of, 8–9
putting it together, 9
Custom cocktail napkins, 97
Custom gift tags, 107
Custom-printed envelope, 24

Dinner party
guest sign-in map, 34–35
hosting tips, 30
menu, 38–39
pinwheel-fold invitation, 32–33
pocket escort card, 36–37

soap label favor gift wrap, 41
table maker, 40
Drink coaster, 66–67

Envelopes, lining of, 10
Envelope size chart, 152
Escort board and cards, 116–117
The Essential Wine Buying Guide, 56

Favor tag, 148–149

Gate-fold invitation and reminder
postcard, 57–59
General invitation guidelines, 150
Gift tags, 21
Guest sign-in and resolution
reminder card, 142–143
Guest sign-in map, 34–35

Holiday CD favor, 134–135
Holiday gathering
holiday CD favor, 134–135
holiday recipe stocking stuffer,
127–129
scrap-paper and tinsel
ornament, 132–133
songbook invitation, 125–126
wish tree sign-in, 130–131
Holiday recipe stocking stuffer,
127–129

Inspiration boards, 30
Invitation guidelines
addressing, 152
calligraphy, 152
envelope size chart, 152
general, 150
wedding, 150
wording, 150–151
Invitation wording guidelines,
150–151

Johnson, Hugh, 56

Letterhead and overlay, 22–23
Lottery ticket favor, 102–103

Mailing label, 24
Menu, 38–39
Menu paddle fan, 50–51
Monograms, 112

New Year's Eve
accordion-fold invitation,
140–141
favor tag, 148–149
guest sign-in and resolution
reminder card, 142–143
hosting tips, 138
party hat menu, 144–145
signature drink sign, 146–147
Note card, 25

Oscar ballot, 73
Outdoor fete
bread bag favor tag, 52–53
hosting tips for, 43
menu paddle fan, 50–51
scroll invitation, 44
signature drink sign and tag,
46–47
utensil display, 48–49

Paperie suite, 151
Party hat menu, 144–145
Party hosting
children and, 12
cocktails serving, 12–13
decoration, 11
dress code, 12
gratitude, 13
lighting, 11
music and entertainment, 13
paperie, use of, 11
seating, 11
style, 11
theme of, 11
Personal stationery
business card, 20
color, 18
custom paperweight, 18
custom-printed envelope, 24
gift tags, 21
letterhead and overlay, 22–23
mailing label, 24
note card, 25
symbols, 18
Pinwheel-fold invitation, 32–33
Pocket escort card, 36–37
Pocket invitation, 108–110
Pocket scrapbook invitation,
98–99
Pocket-sized program book, 115
Pocket Wine Book (Johnson), 56
Pop-up invitation, 82–83
Postage, 10
Postcard guest sign-in, 118–119

Resources, 153–155

Save the date, 111–112
Scrap-paper and tinsel ornament,
132–133
Scroll invitation, 44–45
Shadow box invitation, 71–72
Signature drink sign, 146–147
Signature drink sign and tag,
46–47
Soap label favor gift wrap, 41
Songbook invitation, 125–126
Surprise-party face masks, 90–91

Table maker, 40
Table number menu, 113–114
Tasting note, 60–61
Templates, 156–159
Thank-you note, 107
Treat cone, 76–77
Trivia fan, 74–75

Utensil display, 48–49

Wedding
custom gift tags, 107
escort board and cards, 116–117
hosting tips, 106
monograms, 112
pocket invitation, 108–110
pocket-sized program book, 115
postcard guest sign-in, 118–119
save the date, 111–112
table number menu, 113–114
thank-you note, 107
Wedding invitation guidelines,
150
Wine-glass tag, 65
Wine tasting
blind tasting bottle cover, 62–63
drink coaster, 66–67
gate-fold invitation and
reminder postcard, 57–59
hosting tips, 56
tasting note, 60–61
wine choice and, 54–56
wine-glass tag, 65
wine-tasting program kiosk, 64
Wish tree sign-in, 130–131

KAREN BARTOLOMEI is the founder, owner, and creative director of Grapevine couture paperie and invitation design studio. Her signature designs have graced the pages of *InStyle Weddings, Martha Stewart Weddings,* and BetterHomes&Gardens.com, as well as HGTV's *The Ultimate Wedding Guide* special. She's been hailed as the "Sky's the Limit Stationer" by *Modern Bride* and her invitations called "Paper Perfection" by *Elegant Bride.*
www.grapevinepaperie.com